DEVELOPING READING SKILLS

• **advanced**

2ND EDITION

Susana Gutierrez

Linda Markstein
Louise Hirasawa

HEINLE & HEINLE PUBLISHERS

A Division of Wadsworth, Inc.
Boston, Massachusetts 02116

Library of Congress Cataloging in Publication Data

Markstein, Linda.
    Developing reading skills.

    Summary: A collection of texts emphasizing guided
reading practice and the development of reading speed,
for those who want to strengthen their reading skills
for academic, personal, or career purposes.
    1. English language--Text-books for foreign speakers.
2. Readers--1950-   [1. English language--Textbooks
for foreign speakers.   2. Readers]   I. Hirasawa, Louise.
II. Title.
PE1128.M344   1983   428.6'4   82-22580

Cover and book design adapted from that by Harry Swanson.

ISBN 0-8384-2988-2   First printing: March 1983
Printed in the U.S.A.
                                                          17 18

TABLE OF CONTENTS

To our partnership, two old friends working together

INTRODUCTION

This newly revised text, the second edition of *Developing Reading Skills: Advanced,* is a careful reworking of the earlier edition, which has been in popular use for the past nine years. The second edition of *Developing Reading Skills: Advanced* is designed for adults who want to strengthen their reading skills for academic, personal, or career purposes. These materials have been tested successfully with both native and non-native speakers of English.

This text is part of a reading series by the same authors. It is comparable in difficulty with *Expanding Reading Skills: Advanced,* and it can be used as (a) a predecessor or (b) a replacement for that book. The second edition of *Developing Reading Skills: Advanced* and *Expanding Reading Skills: Advanced* may be preceded by the intermediate texts by the same authors, *Developing Reading Skills: Intermediate* and *Expanding Reading Skills: Intermediate.*

All the texts in this reading series emphasize guided reading practice and the development of reading speed. The readings come from current nonfiction, magazine, and newspaper writing, and they cover a wide subject range in order to expose the reader to the content demands of different types of reading material. They are of graded difficulty and the exercises build upon vocabulary and structures introduced in preceding chapters. Therefore, we recommend that the chapters be presented in the given order if possible. In preparing this text, we have relied on the advice of the experts: ESL students and ESL teachers. Their suggestions have helped us develop these new materials that are challenging and relevant to a wide range of students.

Suggestions for Introducing the Reading

Preparing the student for reading—activating the reader's awareness of preconceptions and expectations—is an essential element in the reading process. The more time spent introducing the reading, the better the results. There are many ways of working into the reading depending upon the goals of the lesson and the needs of the students. In general, we suggest activities of two basic types: A (content predictions) and B (word connotation and tone).

Type A—Content Predictions

1) *Before You Read:* This new pre-reading exercise offers several questions that relate to a major theme of the article. By answering these questions, the students will have developed a framework for reading the article.

2) *Illustrations and Title Clues:* Using only illustrative material (photograph, map, graph) and the title, have the students discuss (a) what they think the subject is; (b) what the picture tells them about the subject; (c) how they feel about the subject, taking care to examine in detail their past experience or knowledge of the subject.

3) *Content Expectations:* Ask the students what they expect the article to say before they read it. (*Note:* It is useful to write these statements on the chalkboard so that they can be re-examined later.)

4) *Point of View:* Ask the students how they think the writer feels about the subject. What view do they expect that he or she will present? Why?

Caution: It is quite natural for people to feel hesitant about hazarding these guesses at first. Care has to be taken to establish an environment of freedom where there is no penalty for being "wrong."

Type B—Word Connotation and Tone

In order to develop an awareness of word connotation and word tone, it can be both useful and challenging to focus on activities of another type. We usually introduce these activities with a word-phrase association. We choose a very general, comprehensive word or phrase related to the reading, write it on the chalkboard, and then ask the students to freely associate any words that come to mind until there are perhaps 30 to 40 words and phrases on the board. Some of the activities available at this point are:

1) *Categorizing:* Have the students make up a few general categories into which these words can be classified.

2) *Word Selection:* Have the students (a) decide which words have negative connotations and which ones positive; (b) choose three words they would like to delete; (c) choose the three words they think are most closely related to the subject. Ask them to explain the reasons for their choices.

Because these activities often generate lively discussion and disagreement, it can be useful to have the students work together in small groups.

There are many more ways to extend these introductory activities to suit the needs of a specific class. Above all, we urge you to vary your approach from time to time to heighten student interest and involvement.

Reading-Skills Development—Suggested Procedures

The reading class should be one in which students will develop useful reading skills. As in the development of any other skill, guided practice over an extended period of time is essential. In the beginning, many students will have difficulty in finishing the articles in the time you suggest, and they will need encouragement and reassurance from you. (*Note:* In this text—unlike the previous edition—we have not recommended specific reading times. We have given reading speeds in words per minute after every reading. You can choose the most appropriate time limit for your class. We found too much variation between classes to recommend specific times.)

The students must learn to stop reading word by word and, instead, read to grasp the general ideas of the article. This can be achieved by careful and consistent use of the rapid reading and comprehension exercises. The transition from specific words to general ideas takes time, and the students need a great deal of encouragement to make this adjustment. They should try to guess the probable meanings of unfamiliar words from their contexts rather than look these words up in the dictionary. (We recommend that dictionaries not be used at all in the classroom.)

The Comprehension Check is separate from the skills exercises. It reflects the major ideas of the article in order to help the students learn to focus on important information. When they read the article a second time, they will be aware, through the Check statements, of what information is important, and they should be encouraged to read with these statements in mind. The Check statements appear in the same order as the presentation of relevant information in the article to aid in recall of that information and to develop a sense of the article's organization.

The second edition of *Developing Reading Skills: Advanced* has been designed for self-instruction as well as for class instruction. (It is possible to purchase an answer key from Newbury House Publishers.) When the text is used for self-instruction, the student will achieve the best results by following the recommended reading procedures.

The rapid reading must be carefully controlled to be effective. We recommend the following steps and suggest that the entire first lesson be done carefully in class to make sure everyone understands the procedure:

1) The students should write the numbers 1 through 10 on both sides of a piece of paper, marking one side "Test 1" and the other side "Test 2."

2) The teacher then announces the amount of time for the first reading of the article. (*Note:* the time should be limited enough to provide challenge.) Students begin reading.

3) While the students are reading, they should be told at intervals how many minutes they have left and which paragraph they should be starting (for example, "Four minutes, paragraph seven"). If a timer clock is used, they can pace themselves.

4) When the teacher announces that time is up, the students *must* stop reading whether or not they have finished the article. (In the beginning, many students *may not* finish the article on the first reading.

5) Students should turn to the Comprehension Check at the end of the chapter, read the statements, and answer true (T) or false (F) on their papers under Test 1. The students should base their answers *only* on information contained in the article.

6) When they have completed the Comprehension Check, students should turn their papers over so that they cannot see Test 1 answers.

7) The teacher should ask the students to reread the article, *starting from the beginning* and skimming quickly over previously read portions.

8) The teacher should announce the time for the second reading. The second reading time should be shorter than the first to encourage scanning for specific information.

9) Repeat Step 3.

10) Repeat Step 5, marking answers under Test 2. Students should not look at their first answers (Test 1) or at the article. (Answers on Test 2 may differ from those on Test 1.)

11) When the reading is particularly long or difficult, a third reading may be necessary. If so, the same procedures should be repeated. Students can fold their test papers to make a fresh surface for Test 3 answers.

12) After the last Comprehension Check, students can work together in small groups to check their answers. Answers should be documented by reference to specific page and paragraph numbers in the article. The emphasis should be on *supporting* the answers. The teacher should encourage well-reasoned interpretations even if they disagree with the given answers.

The Comprehension Check should NEVER be used as a graded quiz. It is the student's personal record of progress and comprehension.

In order to teach another useful reading skill—initial surveying before a second, careful reading—we recommend that Steps 2 and 8 occasionally be reversed. When this is done, the reasons for change in procedure should first be explained to the students to avoid confusion and frustration.

In the beginning, students may show little improvement from Test 1 to Test 2 and, in some cases, scores may even drop. It is particularly important to remind students that it takes time and practice to develop reading skills—just as it does to develop any other skill. They should be encouraged to read the article again outside class for additional practice. With practice over a period of time, scores and comprehension should improve noticeably.

When the article is discussed in class, attention should generally be directed to sentence and paragraph content rather than to individual words. If a key word is unfamiliar, the students should be encouraged to guess the meaning from the context, and they should also be encouraged to see that words can have different meanings in different contexts.

Depending upon the students' needs and ability, there are several ways to review the article orally:

1) The teacher can ask questions about the content.

2) Students can ask each other questions about the content of specific paragraphs.

3) Individual students can explain the meaning of a paragraph in their own words.

4) Students can summarize the article orally as a class exercise.
5) Students can bring related articles to class and give reports on them.

Reading-Skills Development—Exercises

As in the previous edition, the exercises in the second edition of *Developing Reading Skills: Advanced* concentrate on three areas of reading skills development: 1) vocabulary development; 2) structural analysis; 3) relational and inferential analysis. We have added several new exercise types in this edition and have revised some of the other exercises.

• *Analysis of Ideas* (Exercise A) and *Interpretation of Words and Phrases* (Exercise B) develop the student's ability to understand the inner meaning and to discover what is written "between the lines." In these exercises, many types of questions commonly used in schools in English-speaking countries have been included.

• *Analysis of Ideas and Relationships:* This exercise will help the student develop the ability to distinguish between main and supporting ideas, to detect implications, to interpret facts, and to reach conclusions about the major points in the article. In this way, the student can develop skill in active, critical reading.

• *Interpretation of Words and Phrases:* Important (and difficult) sentences, idioms, and concepts are singled out for analysis of meaning. This will lead to better understanding of the article.

• *Reading Reconstruction:* This exercise provides the opportunity to practice some of the newly learned vocabulary in a short, clearly constructed paragraph. After reading the paragraph several times, the student can then try to restate the content of the paragraph (either orally or in writing). Another variation on this exercise is to read the paragraph to the students several times, and then ask the students to reconstruct the content based upon their aural comprehension of the paragraph.

• *Synonyms:* Vocabulary is extended through a study of word similarities in the context of the reading topic.

• *Word Forms:* Vocabulary is developed through a study of word families. A chart of forms accompanies each exercise.

• *Participles:* The use of participles as adjectives is examined to provide another tool for comprehension.

• *Determiners* and *Prepositions* concentrate on particular areas of language difficulty while using content from the article.

• *Sentence Construction* draws attention to various possibilities for creating sentences in English. Students are asked to make a meaningful sentence out of a group of words in the order in which they are given. Students should be encouraged to try for variety in their sentences.

The new exercise types include:

- *Cloze:* In order to build an awareness of syntactic and semantic cues in language (specifically in print), the student is asked to fill in blanks in a passage from multiple choice selections. The appropriate filler will satisfy the semantic and syntactic constraints of the passage. Where more than one filler is possible, students will learn to consider register in making their choice.

- *Antonyms:* Vocabulary is extended through a study of word contrasts in meaningful context.

- *Punctuation:* To highlight common punctuation patterns and options, students are asked to restore capital letters, commas, and periods to a paragraph.

- *Graph Reading* and *Map Reading:* These exercises focus on the skills needed for reading various types of graphs and maps.

- *Dictionary Skills:* These reviews of dictionary skills will reinforce for students the many uses of their dictionary and the need to examine word meanings with care.

- *Sentence Paraphrase:* Students explore various ways of conveying the same ideas.

Review Examinations

A short review examination appears after every four chapters.

Using the Reading Text to Reinforce Other Language Development Activities

In many English as a Foreign Language and English as a Second Language programs, reading is taught in combination with other language-development activities. Consequently, teachers often ask us how our texts can be used to reinforce grammar, sentence structure, and composition activities. We believe that intellectual content is an essential component of real language activities no matter what they may be, and our readers provide content that can be effectively used for a variety of purposes.

Let us suppose that the grammar focus in a lesson is the past tense. Most of the readings in this book can be discussed using past tense:

- *What were some of the myths about the American grandmother?*

- *What were some of the differences the author mentioned between American grandmothers of today and the stereotype of grandmothers?*

In the discussion-composition topics near the end of each chapter, we have tried to phrase the topics in such a way as to naturally elicit different verb tenses. These topics may give you ideas for how to focus discussions in order to give practice in specific grammar elements.

If the aim of the lesson is to give practice in pronunciation and intonation, sentences from the reading (or perhaps the comprehension check) can be used. This can lend meaning to the practice.

The readings can be used very easily to teach sentence patterns—and to prove that the various sentence patterns of English are actually used! All the readings provide repeated examples of the sentence patterns.

We have always believed that the reading should be taught together with composition and that the best results come from developing these skills together: good readers are good writers are good readers. . . . We have tried to provide interesting, fully developed composition topics in order to guide students in their compositions. These composition topics have proved particularly effective when the students have been given ample opportunity to discuss them before they begin writing.

1

Before you read, here are some questions to think about:

— Do you think that overpopulation is a problem today? Why do you think so? What evidence have you seen of this problem?

— Have you ever lived in a place that was clearly overpopulated? What were some of the problems that developed?

— What can be done to slow population growth?

— Do you think the government should be involved in population control? Why? Or why not?

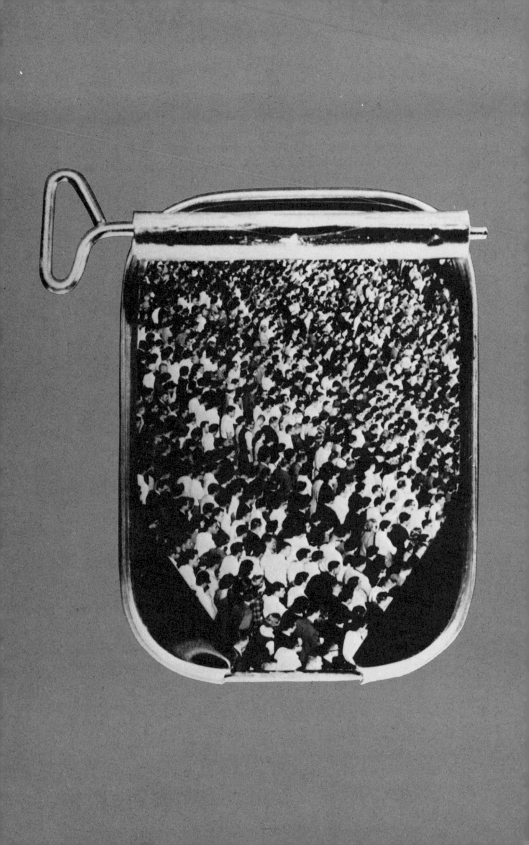

TWO BILLION MORE PEOPLE BY CENTURY'S END

[By the end of this century, it is expected that the world's population will reach 6.4 billion people. This article discusses some problems that will likely occur when so many people must compete for space, food, and jobs.]

1   The world's exploding population signals even more growing pains ahead for already crowded areas. A new United Nations study forecasts that by the year 2000, 2 billion persons will be added to the 4.4 billion in the world today.

2   Even more troubling than the increasing number of inhabitants are the projections of where they will be concentrated. The study by Rafael M. Salas, executive director of the U.N. Fund for Population Activities, notes that by the year 2000:

• Nearly 80 percent of all people will live in less developed countries, many hard pressed to support their present populations. That compares with 70 percent today.

• In many of these Third World lands, metropolises will become centers of concentrated urban poverty because of a flood of migration from rural areas.

• The bulging centers, mainly in Asia and Latin America, will increasingly become fertile fields for social unrest. More young residents of the urban clusters will be better educated, unemployed, and demanding of a better lifestyle.

3   To slow the rush to urban centers, countries will have to vastly expand opportunities in the countryside, the study suggests. Says Salas: "The solution to the urban problem lies as much in the rural areas as in the cities themselves."

4   Worldwide, the number of large cities will multiply. Now 26 cities have 5 million or more residents each and a combined population of 252 million. By the end of the decade, the number will escalate to 60, with an estimated total of almost 650 million people.

5   In the more developed countries of North America and Europe, however, the growth trend for two decades has been away from urban clusters. In the United States, for instance, only three urban areas—centered on New York, Los Angeles, and Chicago—are among the top 25 population agglomerates in the world. By 2000, only two, New York and Los Angeles, will be in the top 25.

6   Ray of hope: The world population now is growing by 1.8 percent a year; by 2000, the rate is expected to drop to 1.6 percent as individual women have fewer children in their lifetimes.

TURN TO COMPREHENSION CHECK AT END OF CHAPTER

350 words

READING TIMES:	READING SPEED:
1st reading _____ minutes	4 minutes = 88 wpm
2nd reading _____ minutes	3 minutes = 117 wpm
	2 minutes = 175 wpm

A. **Analysis of Ideas and Relationships: Circle the letter next to the best answer.**

1. The main idea of this article is that:
   a. already crowded areas should expect more problems as the world's population increases.
   b. Third World countries should encourage their citizens to become farmers.
   c. people all over the world should have more children.

   Please explain your answer.

2. In paragraph 2, all the listed items are:
   a. examples of the current world population.
   b. Rafael M. Salas's personal opinions about the future.
   c. conclusions reached by the U.N. study.

3. According to paragraph 2, the first listed item ("Nearly 80 percent ... , that a _____ of people will live in less developed countries by the year 2000.
   a. larger percentage
   b. smaller percentage
   c. similar percentage

4. Please read the section beginning with "The bulging centers..." in paragraph 2. The second sentence explains:
   a. why young people are better educated.
   b. why social unrest is likely to occur.
   c. why there are more young residents.

5. In paragraph 3, **although he doesn't directly say it,** Mr. Salas would probably agree that:
   a. there is no solution to the urban problems.
   b. governments should encourage people to live in the urban centers.
   c. people should be encouraged to live in rural areas.

   Please explain your answer.

6. In paragraph 4 ("By the end of the decade, the number will escalate to 60, . . ."), **60** refers to:
   a. people.
   b. cities.
   c. estimated total.

7. Paragraph 5 implies, **but does not directly state,** that in North America and Europe:
   a. growth is slowing down in large cities.
   b. large cities are growing rapidly.
   c. urban clusters are disappearing.

   Please explain your answer.

8. According to paragraph 5, what will happen to Chicago by the year 2000?
   a. Chicago will be the biggest city in the United States.
   b. Chicago will no longer be an urban area.
   c. Chicago will no longer be among the largest 25 cities in the world.

9. The subject of paragraph 6 is:
   a. the birthrate in the year 2000.
   b. individual women.
   c. the rate of population growth.

10. This article:
   a. explains the difficulties that are caused by the exploding population.
   b. suggests some solutions to the problems caused by the exploding population.
   c. both (a) and (b)

B. Interpretation of Words and Phrases: Circle the letter next to the best answer.

1. "The world's exploding population signals **even more** growing pains. . . ."
   a. quiet
   b. regular
   c. additional

2. "The world's exploding population signals even more **growing pains**. . . ."
   a. minor pains
   b. difficulties that occur when something is expanding or growing
   c. problems in providing enough food for a large population

3. According to paragraph 1, what will the world population be by the year 2000?
   a. 6.4 billion people
   b. 2 billion people
   c. 4.4 billion people

4. **Nearly** 80 percent of all people will live in less developed countries.
   a. living near each other
   b. more than
   c. almost

5. Many countries **are hard pressed** to support their present populations.
   a. are trying harder
   b. are finding it difficult
   c. are looking for new ways

6. Many **Third World** lands will become centers of urban poverty.
   a. one-third of the world's population
   b. industrialized
   c. less developed

7. "The bulging centers will increasingly become fertile fields for social unrest." This means that:
   a. the crowded cities will be a likely place for revolutions to take place.
   b. many people will become farmers because they are dissatisfied with city life.
   c. residents of large cities will have lots of opportunities for a better life.

8. By the end of the decade, the **estimated total** will be almost 650 million people.
   a. approximate number
   b. exact number
   c. wild guess

9. According to paragraph 5, "By 2000, only two, New York and Los Angeles, will be in the top 25."

The **2000** refers to:

a. cities.

b. people.

c. the year.

The **25** refers to:

a. cities.

b. people.

c. the year.

10. "The rate is expected to drop to 1.6 percent as individual women have fewer children in **their** lifetimes." **Their** refers to:

a. children.

b. women.

c. rate.

C. **Synonyms: From this list, choose a synonym for the word in bold type in each sentence. Use appropriate tenses for verbs and singular or plural forms for nouns.**

to crowd together	must	to rise
to hurry	pattern	total
group	to predict	swollen
inhabitant		

1. This study **forecasts** a shift in population growth. (___*predicts*___)

2. Thirty percent of Japan's population **is concentrated** around Tokyo.

3. The **bulging** centers of population will cause problems for Third World countries.

4. The **residents** of my city are concerned about pollution and housing problems.

5. Cities near each other will grow until they form urban **clusters.**

6. Many countries **have to** expand opportunities in the countryside.

7. Population problems **have escalated** quickly in the past few years.

8. The worldwide **trend** is towards smaller families.

9. The people **are rushing** to urban centers.

10. The **combined** population of the 26 largest cities is 252 million.

D. Prepositions and Verb-Completers: Write any appropriate preposition or verb-completer in the blank spaces.

1. __By__ the year 2000, 2 billion people will be added __to__ the 4.4 billion __in__ the world today.

2. Mr. Salas is the executive director _____ the U.N. Fund _____ Population Activities.

3. Nearly 80 percent _____ all people will live _____ less developed countries.

4. That compares _____ 70 percent today.

5. There will be a flood _____ migration _____ rural areas.

6. Countries will have _____ expand opportunities _____ the countryside.

7. The number will escalate _____ 60, _____ an estimated total _____ 650 million.

8. The growth trend _____ two decades has been away _____ urban clusters.

9. By 2000, only New York and Los Angeles will be _____ the top 25.

10. The world population now is growing _____ 1.8 percent a year.

E. **Determiners:** Write any appropriate determiner in the following blanks. If no determiner is necessary, write an "*X*" in the blank. (Some examples of determiners are: a, the, this, that, these, those, my, your, our, his, her, their, its, some, any, no, one, two, etc.)

Worldwide, __*the*__ number of __X__ large cities will
                    (1)   (2)
multiply. Now _____ 26 cities have _____ 5 million or
                      (3)   (4)
_____ more residents each and _____ combined population
     (5)   (6)
of _____ 252 million. By _____ end of _____ decade,
      (7)   (8)   (9)
_____ number will escalate to _____ 60, with _____
    (10)   (11)   (12)
estimated total of _____ almost 650 million _____ people. In
                        (13)   (14)
_____ more developed countries of _____ North America and
    (15)   (16)
_____ Europe, however, _____ growth trend has been away
    (17)   (18)
from _____ urban clusters.
          (19)

F. Graph Reading: Look at the population graph and answer these questions.

1. This graph shows:
   a. the biggest population clusters in 1980.
   b. the biggest population clusters in 2000.
   c. both (a) and (b)

2. In 1980, the two largest population clusters were:
   a. New York-New Jersey and Tokyo-Yokohama.
   b. Mexico City and São Paulo.
   c. Mexico City and New York-New Jersey.

3. In 2000, the two largest population clusters will be:
   a. Mexico City and São Paulo.
   b. New York-New Jersey and Tokyo-Yokohama.
   c. Tokyo-Yokohama and Mexico City.

4. In the year 2000, _Mexico City_ will have the largest population and
   Milan will have the smallest. (Fill in the blanks.)

5. In the year 2000, will any of the clusters have **less** population than they do
   today?
   a. No.
   b. Yes. _London & Rhine-Ruhr_
   If you answer yes, which ones?

6. Circle all the cities in which the population will more than double between
   1980 and 2000.
   a. New York   e. Bombay   h. Milan
   b. Mexico City   f. Cairo   i. Manila
   c. Rio de Janeiro   g. Djakarta   j. Bogotá
   d. Seoul

7. In 2000, New York and _____ will have almost the same size
   population:
   a. São Paulo
   b. Los Angeles-Long Beach
   c. Shanghai

8. On the graph, there is a small number in parentheses after each population.
   a. What does this number refer to?
      1. The rank of that cluster in the graph.
      2. How old each cluster is.
      3. The population in the year 2000.
   b. Why does this number change on the "Year 2000" side of the graph?
      1. Because the populations have stayed the same.
      2. Because the clusters are made up of several cities.
      3. Because the rank of each cluster has changed.

Biggest Population Clusters—Now and in Year 2000

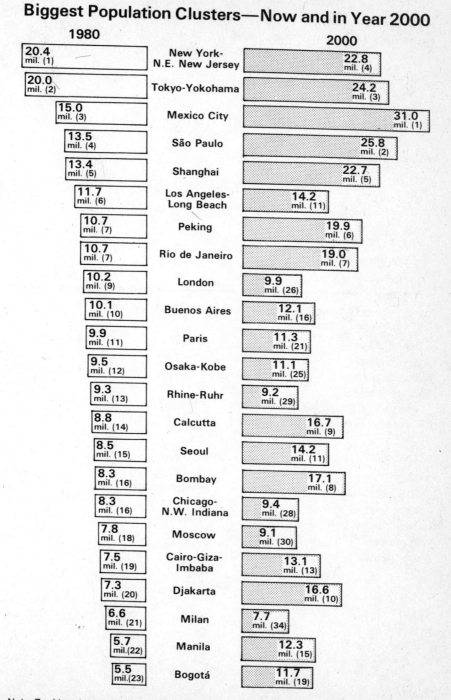

1980		2000
20.4 mil. (1)	New York- N.E. New Jersey	22.8 mil. (4)
20.0 mil. (2)	Tokyo-Yokohama	24.2 mil. (3)
15.0 mil. (3)	Mexico City	31.0 mil. (1)
13.5 mil. (4)	São Paulo	25.8 mil. (2)
13.4 mil. (5)	Shanghai	22.7 mil. (5)
11.7 mil. (6)	Los Angeles- Long Beach	14.2 mil. (11)
10.7 mil. (7)	Peking	19.9 mil. (6)
10.7 mil. (7)	Rio de Janeiro	19.0 mil. (7)
10.2 mil. (9)	London	9.9 mil. (26)
10.1 mil. (10)	Buenos Aires	12.1 mil. (16)
9.9 mil. (11)	Paris	11.3 mil. (21)
9.5 mil. (12)	Osaka-Kobe	11.1 mil. (25)
9.3 mil. (13)	Rhine-Ruhr	9.2 mil. (29)
8.8 mil. (14)	Calcutta	16.7 mil. (9)
8.5 mil. (15)	Seoul	14.2 mil. (11)
8.3 mil. (16)	Bombay	17.1 mil. (8)
8.3 mil. (16)	Chicago- N.W. Indiana	9.4 mil. (28)
7.8 mil. (18)	Moscow	9.1 mil. (30)
7.5 mil. (19)	Cairo-Giza- Imbaba	13.1 mil. (13)
7.3 mil. (20)	Djakarta	16.6 mil. (10)
6.6 mil. (21)	Milan	7.7 mil. (34)
5.7 mil.(22)	Manila	12.3 mil. (15)
5.5 mil.(23)	Bogotá	11.7 mil. (19)

Note: Rankings in parentheses. Other population clusters in 2000 and their rank—Madras, 12.9 million (14th); Bangkok-Thonburi, 11.9 million (17th) and Karachi, 11.8 million (18th).

9. What does the note at the bottom of the graph tell you?
   a. Not all the cities in the world are listed on the graph.
   b. The three cities mentioned in the note will rank in this graph in the year 2000.
   c. Bangkok-Thonburi is not on the graph because it is only seventeenth in rank.

10. Look at the chart "Biggest Urban Areas of Earlier Times." In 1360 B.C., most of the world's largest cities were located in:
    a. the West.
    b. the Middle East.
    c. the East.

11. Where did the basic data for these charts come from?
    a. United Nations.
    b. USN&WR charts.
    c. Other sources.

    How do you know?

Biggest Urban Areas of Earlier Times

1360 B.C.

Thebes (Greece)	100,000
Memphis (Egypt)	74,000
Babylon (Iraq)	54,000
Chengchow (China)	40,000
Khattushas (Turkey)	40,000

1000

Cordoba (Spain)	450,000
Constantinople (Turkey)	450,000
Kaifeng (China)	400,000
Sian (China)	300,000
Kyoto (Japan)	200,000

1600

Peking (China)	706,000
Constantinople (Turkey)	700,000
Agra (India)	500,000
Cairo (Egypt)	400,000
Osaka (Japan)	400,000

1925

New York	7,774,000
London	7,742,000
Tokyo	5,300,000
Paris	4,800,000
Berlin	4,013,000
Chicago	3,564,000
Ruhr	3,400,000
Buenos Aires	2,410,000
Osaka	2,219,000
Philadelphia	2,085,000
Vienna	1,862,000
Boston	1,773,000
Moscow	1,764,000
Manchester	1,725,000
Birmingham (England)	1,700,000
Shanghai	1,500,000
Leningrad	1,430,000
Glasgow	1,396,000
Detroit	1,394,000
Calcutta	1,390,000
Hamburg	1,369,000
Budapest	1,318,000
Peking	1,266,000
Rio de Janeiro	1,240,000
Liverpool	1,235,000

Homework

G. **Word Forms:** Choose the correct word form to fit into each sentence
referring to the chart as necessary. Use appropriate verb tenses, singular or
plural forms for nouns, and passive voice where necessary.

Noun	Verb	Adjective	Adverb
center	to center to centralize	central	centrally
demand	to demand	demanding	
expanse expansion	to expand	expanding expanded	
explosion	to explode	explosive	explosively
growth	to grow	growing grown	
hope	to hope	hopeful hopeless	hopefully hopelessly
increase	to increase	increasing increased	increasingly
projection projector	to project	projected	
society	to socialize	social sociable	socially
solution	to solve	solvable	

1. **explosion, to explode, explosive, explosively**
   a. There was a terrible _explosion_ and then we saw the smoke.
   b. The storm began suddenly with _explosive_ force.
   c. The storm began _explosively_ .
   d. Many countries have holidays on which fireworks are _exploded_ .

2. **growth, to grow, growing, grown**
   a. My two _grown_ children have both finished college.
   b. _Growing_ children need good nourishment.
   c. The _growth_ of world population is being studied.
   d. As cities _grow_ , there will be a need for more housing and
      transportation.

3. increase, to increase, increasing, increased, increasingly
   a. The population of the world _____ at a rapid rate now.
   b. The problems of urban clusters will become _____ difficult.
   c. The last census reported an _____ in the number of households in my city.
   d. An _____ number of women are having fewer children.
   e. With my _____ ability in English, I was able to get a good job.

4. projection, projector, to project, projected
   a. Do you think that all the *projection* for the year 2000 are accurate?
   b. Many people try *to project* what their lives will be like in the future.
   c. Mr. and Mrs. Ramirez like to make family movies and show them on a movie *projector* at home.
   d. The budget was voted down because the *projected* figures were too high.

5. center, to center, to centralize, central, centrally
   a. The lawyer has a *centrally* located office downtown.
   b. If you want the two sides to be even, you must measure from the *center*.
   c. The *central* point of this article is that the world population is increasing.
   d. First, you must *to center* the pattern on the paper. Then you can cut it.
   e. The Omega Company has branches all over England, but last year it *centralized* all its records in the head office in London.

6. society, to socialize, social, sociable, socially
   a. The city built a *social* center with a swimming pool and gymnasium.
   b. Rita is very *sociable*. She loves to go to parties.
   c. Is it _____ acceptable to eat fried chicken with your fingers?
   d. People who like _____ generally belong to clubs.
   e. For a _____ to function well, people must obey the laws.

7. demand, to demand, demanding
   a. I *demand* to speak to the manager!
   b. Judge Lee has a very *demanding* job on the High Court.
   c. The company met the *demands* of the employees for better insurance benefits.

8. **expanse, expansion, to expand, expanding, expanded**
   a. The Sahara Desert is a large _____ of sand in North Africa.
   b. The _____ opportunities in the computer industry are providing new jobs.
   c. Mrs. Van Vleit will expand her knowledge of computers by taking some classes next winter.
   d. The company's _____ facilities provided more warehouse space.
   e. The company's _____ will provide new jobs.

9. **solution, to solve, solvable**
   a. Every problem is solvable _____ , but it might not be easy to find the answer.
   b. Many problems are solved already, but new ones always arise.
   c. There must be a solution to this problem.

10. **hope, to hope, hopeful, hopeless, hopefully, hopelessly**
    a. This study is _____ that the rate of population increase will slow down.
    b. Despite her problems, she looked to the future _____ .
    c. The family felt so _____ when their car broke down on the highway.
    d. They stood _____ at the side of the road.
    e. I _____ to see you again soon.
    f. My _____ is that all your plans will succeed.

H. Sentence Construction: Use each group of words in the order and form given to construct an original, meaningful sentence. Various sentences can be made from each group of words.

1. *Example:* world's population, growing pains, already crowded.

   The increase in the world's population is causing growing pains in already crowded countries.

   Can the world's population cope with its growing pains if already crowded countries continue to grow?

2. nearly 80 percent, people, less developed countries

3. countries, vastly expand, opportunities, countryside

4. growth, trend, away, urban clusters

5. rate, drop, individual women, fewer children

I. Topics for Discussion and Composition

1. The world's population is now growing by a quarter of a million people a day. Do you think the earth can accommodate so many people or is the world becoming overpopulated? Why do you think so? Please explain your answer with several examples.

2. If you think the world can accommodate an expanding population, what are some problems that will arise? What will need to be done so all the people will have enough food, housing, jobs, and other necessities?

3. If you think the world is becoming overcrowded, how would you stop this growth? How could you encourage people to have fewer children? Should governments give benefits to people who have fewer children (e.g., lower taxes, education benefits)? Why or why not?

4. "To slow the rush to urban centers, countries will have to vastly expand opportunities in the countryside." Can you think of a few examples of the kind of opportunities that could be provided in the countryside? Please explain your ideas.

5. Is your country having any problems because of population growth? If so, discuss some of the problems that concern your country. If not, do you see any indications that overpopulation will become a problem in the future?

6. What are the differences between population growth problems in developed and in less developed countries?

7. How does the photograph illustrate subjects mentioned in this article?

J. Reading Reconstruction: Read this paragraph as many times as you can in three minutes. Then, with your book closed, restate the ideas in writing as clearly and as completely as you can. Your teacher will write key words on the chalkboard. You do not have to use all of the words. They are offered only to help you remember. The emphasis in Reading Reconstruction is on comprehension and restatement of *ideas*. Make sure that your sentences are meaningful and that your grammatical structure is correct. (*Note:* If you wish to practice this type of exercise outside class, you can do so easily by using short paragraphs taken from newspapers or magazines, following the above instructions.)

Population Growth in China

Since 1920, the population of China has doubled. With over one billion people today, China accounts for 23 percent of the world's population. This increase is the greatest problem in China's plans to modernize itself. In order to solve this population problem, China has begun a "one child" policy. This means that married couples have to limit their families to one child even if they would like to have more children. This policy has been most effective in the big cities where residents live in crowded apartments. In the countryside, however, the farmers say they are hard pressed to limit their families to one child since they need more children to help with the farm work. Factories and farms reward "one child" families with free medical care, better housing, extra vacations, and cash bonuses. If couples have more than one child, they lose these benefits, and their salaries may be cut by 10 percent or even more. This trend to one child families should slow down China's population growth to a rate of 1.3 percent per year.

Key words (to be written on the chalkboard):

population	increase	"one child" policy	reward
doubled	problem	limit	benefits
one billion	modernize	countryside	trend
23 percent	solve	hard pressed	rate

Comprehension Check

On a separate piece of paper, write the numbers 1 through 10 on both sides. Mark one side "Test 1" and the other side "Test 2." Read each statement and decide whether it is true or false. Write "T" after true statements and "F" after false statements under Test 1. After you have finished the comprehension check, turn Test 1 face down. Then read the article again and do the comprehension check again under Test 2. Base your answers on the information in this article *only,* even if you disagree with what the author said.

1. This article states the conclusions of a United Nations study.

2. By the year 2000, there will be 4.4 billion people in the world.

3. The world's population explosion is occurring mostly in the less developed countries.

4. Large cities will contain fewer poor people by the year 2000.

5. Residents of Third World urban centers will have a better life because they are well educated and have jobs.

6. This article suggests that countries will have to expand opportunities in the countryside.

7. Cities in Asia and Latin America will probably experience more and more social problems.

8. Today 60 cities already have populations of 5 million or more.

9. In North America, population growth has been away from urban centers.

10. According to this article, the rate of population growth will drop because women are having fewer children.

2

Before you read, here are some questions to think about:

— What does getting an education mean to you?

— How do you expect having an education will change your life?

— Will you have to make sacrifices for your education? If so, what are the sacrifices and why do you have to make them?

— Will having an education separate you from your family and friends in any way?

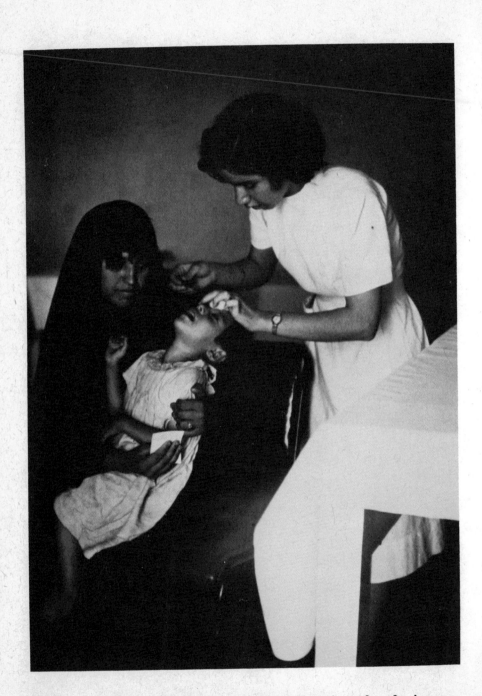

Today, women in the Middle East are entering a variety of professions.

ISLAMIC CUSTOMS
LIMIT KUWAITI WOMEN

1   "Islamic law is very good for the equality of women," said Dr. Badria al-Awadhi, Kuwait's first woman law professor, "but the people who interpret the Islamic law are men. And they try to do it in a way that is right for them and not for us."

2   "Us" are the women of Kuwait, many of whom are becoming educated, some of whom have professional careers, and none of whom is allowed to vote. Like women in other westernizing Third World societies, Kuwaiti females are demanding their rights and overturning conventions. But in a country where until recently women were shrouded behind black veils, progress can be agonizingly slow.

3   "We are the sacrificial generation," Dr. al-Awadhi said. "We wanted to prove ourselves as women, that we are equal, that we could do the same job as men. But at the same time, we lost one thing—the family. Most of us in this position, I could say, are not married."

4   Dr. Badria al-Awadhi, the first female dean of Kuwait University's School of Law and Shariah (Islamic law), is in a profession totally dominated by men. At 35, she is responsible for a law school faculty of 42 men. With a doctorate in international law and a wide record of publications, Dr. al-Awadhi said her male colleagues, many of whom are non-Kuwaitis, didn't resist that much.

5   But like all pioneers, she paid a price. "I feel that I gave up making my own family for my degree," said the doctor of law at her desk in the cavernous office. "I had to balance two things—a husband and children or this career. I prefer to be a career woman. Men my age didn't want to marry a woman who was on the same level as them," she said while her two male secretaries brought papers to sign. "They took those lower than them. Society in the Arab east looked on a man very badly if his wife was on the same level as him."

6   Educated women even found difficulties with prospective mothers-in-law. "When you marry here, you marry the whole family," said Dr. al-Awadhi. "The husband usually took the wife to live with his family. So if you're a man and you have a very educated wife and your mother doesn't know how to read—well, it is very difficult."

7   The problems she faced may not confront Dr. al-Awadhi's female students. Females make up 51 percent of Kuwait University's students and they attend classes wearing the latest fashions of Paris and Rome. "Before, a man had to choose between educated and non-educated," Dr. al-Awadhi said. "Now almost all young women are educated. A man doesn't have a choice anymore."

8   Dr. al-Awadhi was one of six children of a wealthy Kuwaiti trader, who died when she was young. Her elder brother, now Kuwait's minister of health (1980), pushed her and her sisters to take up a profession. When the parliament is in session, Dr. al-Awadhi lobbies the all-male leadership of Kuwait to grant women the right to vote and hold office.

TURN TO COMPREHENSION CHECK AT END OF CHAPTER

500 words

READING TIMES:
1st reading _____ minutes
2nd reading _____ minutes

READING SPEED:
5 minutes = 100 wpm
4 minutes = 125 wpm
3 minutes = 166 wpm
2 minutes = 250 wpm

A. **Analysis of Ideas and Relationships: Circle the letter next to the best answer.**

1. This article is about:
   a. Islamic life in modern-day Kuwait.
   b. social changes in Kuwait.
   c. problems faced by professional women in Kuwait.

   Please explain your answer.

2. "Islamic law is very good for the equality of women," said Dr. Badria al-Awadhi, Kuwait's first woman law professor, "but the people who interpret the Islamic law are men. And **they** try to do it in a way that is right for **them** and not for **us**."

   They and **them** refer to: **Us** refers to:
   a. people.   a. people.
   b. men.   b. men.
   c. women.   c. women.

   Please explain your answer.

3. Paragraph 3, sentence 1 (" 'We are the sacrificial generation,' Dr. al-Awadhi said.") is explained by:
   a. paragraph 3, sentences 2, 3, and 4.
   b. paragraph 4.
   c. paragraph 2.

   Please explain your answer.

4. Dr. Badria al-Awadhi's remarks are particularly important because:
   a. she is an international lawyer and an expert in Islamic law.
   b. she is a Kuwaiti woman.
   c. she is a Kuwaiti woman and a leader in a totally male dominated field.

   Please explain your answer.

5. Why is Dr. Badria al-Awadhi referred to as a pioneer?
   a. Because she is one of the first highly educated Kuwaiti women.
   b. Because she has an adventurous spirit.
   c. Because she is not afraid to try new things.

6. Paragraphs 5 and 6 are written primarily in the past tense. Why?
   a. To indicate that Kuwaiti society is changing and the experiences of Dr. al-Awadhi and women of her generation may not confront young, educated women in Kuwait today.
   b. To indicate that Kuwaiti society has not changed and that young, educated women in Kuwait face the same difficulties today as Dr. al-Awadhi and women of her generation did.
   c. To indicate that Kuwaiti society may change in the future, but it has not changed up to now.

   Please explain your answer, concentrating on the general meaning and function of the past tense.

7. Why do you think the writer mentions that female students today "attend classes wearing the latest fashions of Paris and Rome"?
   a. To show that they are well dressed.
   b. To show that other social customs are changing too.
   c. To show how wealthy Kuwaitis are.

   Please explain your answer.

8. Which statement is NOT true?
   a. Social customs in Kuwait are changing.
   b. There is resistance to social change in Kuwait.
   c. Social change occurs quickly.

   Why do you think so?

9. Paragraph 8, sentence 3, shows that Dr. al-Awadhi:
   a. is involved in the government.
   b. is interested in politics and would like to hold a political office.
   c. is active in women's rights in general.

10. The writer of this article is:
    a. sympathetic to educated Kuwaiti women.
    b. sympathetic to the position of Kuwaiti men.
    c. critical of the position of educated women in Kuwait.

Why do you think so?

B. **Interpretation of Words and Phrases: Circle the letter next to the best answer.**

1. " 'We are the sacrificial generation,' Dr. al-Awadhi said." This means that the first generation of educated Kuwaiti women:
   a. was not successful in receiving professional acceptance from men.
   b. had to give up something: having a family.
   c. was able to attain both personal and professional goals.

2. In the phrase, "Kuwait University's School of Law and Shariah (Islamic law)," why is Islamic law written in parentheses?
   a. To show that Shariah and Islamic law mean the same thing.
   b. To show that Islamic law is a division of Shariah.
   c. To show that Islamic law is less important than Shariah.

3. "But like all pioneers, she **paid a price.**" **Paid a price** means she:
   a. had to give up something important to reach her goal.
   b. had to pay a lot of money for her education.
   c. sacrificed too much for her goal.

4. Dr. al-Awadhi's statement, "I feel that I gave up making my own family for my degree," means that she:
   a. succeeded in combining family and career.
   b. sacrificed having a family in order to have a career.
   c. did not want to have a family.

5. "Men my age didn't want to marry a woman who was on the same **level** as them . . . ." **Level** here refers to:
   a. education level.
   b. social class level.
   c. economic level.

6. "They took those lower than them." This means that Kuwaiti men married women who were:
   a. from a lower social class.
   b. not as educated as they were.
   c. from poor families.

7. "When **you** marry here, **you** marry the whole family." Who is **you** in this context?
   a. The person Dr. al-Awadhi is speaking to, the writer of this article.
   b. Kuwaiti women.
   c. Kuwaiti men and women.

   Please explain your answer. Refer back to paragraph 6 for context.

8. In paragraph 7, the statement that "a man doesn't have a choice anymore" means that:
   a. Kuwaiti men can't choose whom they want to marry now.
   b. Kuwaiti men, whether they like it or not, will have to marry educated Kuwaiti women because most Kuwaiti women are educated now.
   c. Kuwaiti men will never marry educated Kuwaiti women because they prefer non-educated women.

9. "Her elder brother . . . **pushed** her and her sisters to **take up a profession**." **Pushed** means:
   a. encouraged.
   b. forced.
   c. shoved.

   Take up a profession means:
   a. to marry someone with a profession.
   b. to study to become a professional in some field.
   c. to respect people in professions.

C. **Synonyms:** From this list choose a synonym for the word in bold type in each sentence. Use appropriate tenses for verbs and singular or plural forms for nouns.

co-workers (in a profession)	painfully	to try to persuade
to be controlled by	huge	to be hidden
to give	to face	to comprise
to protest		

1. In Kuwait, women **were shrouded** behind veils until recently, and women continue to wear veils in places like Iran and Saudi Arabia.

2. Dr. al-Awadhi has achieved great success in a field **dominated by** men.

3. She said her male **colleagues** did not oppose her appointment.

4. They didn't **resist** that much.

5. Now she conducts her business in a **cavernous** office.

6. Women now **make up** 51 percent of Kuwait University's students.

7. Dr. al-Awadhi said her female students may not have to **confront** the problems she faced as a professional woman.

8. & 9. Dr. al-Awadhi **lobbies** the leadership of Kuwait to **grant** women the right to vote and hold office.

10. Kuwaiti women are making progress, but sometimes progress can be **agonizingly** slow.

D. **Prepositions and Verb-Completers:** Write any appropriate preposition or verb-completer in the blank spaces.

1. Dr. al-Awadhi said, "Islamic law is very good _____ the equality _____ women."

2. Men, the interpreters _____ Islamic law, try _____ interpret it _____ a way that is right _____ them and not _____ women.

3. Women _____ Kuwait are not allowed _____ vote.

4. Dr. al-Awadhi is _____ a field totally dominated _____ men.

5. Most _____ the women _____ her position are not married.

6. Women like Dr. al-Awadhi have paid a price _____ their success.

7. They have had _____ give _____ having their own families.

8. Now women make _____ 51 percent _____ Kuwait University's students.

9. Dr. al-Awadhi was one _____ six children _____ a wealthy Kuwaiti trader.

10. Her elder brother encouraged her and her sisters _____ take _____ a profession.

E. Cloze Exercise: Select the best word to fill in each blank. Sometimes there may be more than one possible answer.

"Islamic law is very good for the equality of women," said Dr. Badria

al-Awadhi, Kuwait's first woman law professor, "but the people who

interpret the Islamic law are men. And they try to (1)_____ it
(make—do—write)

in a way (2)_____ is right for them (3)_____ not for us."
(that—who—whom)   (and—or—so)

"Us" (4)_____ the women of Kuwait, (5)_____ of
(is—are—were)   (many—none—some)

whom are becoming (6)_____, some of whom have
(rich—angry—educated)

(7)_____ careers and none of (8)_____ is
(professional—good—new)   (who—whom—which)

allowed to vote.

(9)_____ women in other westernizing
(Similar—Like—When)

(10)_____ World societies, Kuwaiti
(industrial—Third—eastern)

(11)_____ are demanding their rights (12)_____
(females—males—people)   (by—and—but)

overturning conventions. But in (13)_____ country where until
(the—that—a)

recently (14)_____ were shrouded behind black
(people—men—women)

(15)_____, progress can be agonizingly slow.
(dresses—veils—coats)

F. Dictionary Skills Review: A dictionary has many uses in addition to helping you understand the meanings of words. It can help you with spelling, pronunciation, accent, the division of words into syllables, idiomatic expressions, and the relationship of words to each other. Look at the page from a dictionary on page 29 and answer these questions.

1. a. The **guide words** at the top of the page (**doggerel** and **Dominican**) show the first and last words on that page. By looking at only the guide words you can quickly tell which words would appear on that page. Circle the words that would appear on a page with **doggerel/Dominican** for guide words.

   doll   domestic   doctor   dominion   dome   door

   b. If the guide words were **lighten/like**, which words would appear on the page?

   light   lightning   likely   ligneous   lilt   liking

2. On this dictionary page look at the first word: **doggerel**. The word is separated into three syllables: dog•ger•el. How is **domesticate** divided into syllables? Circle the correct answer.

   dom•es•ti•cate   do•mes•ti•cate   do•me•stic•ate

3. Look these words up in your dictionary and rewrite them to show how they are divided into syllables. (**Note:** If you need to divide a word at the end of a line, always divide it between syllables.)

   professional _____   generation _____
   family _____   demand _____
   liberation _____   sacrifice _____
   cavernous _____   colleague _____

4. The syllables give you clues for pronunciation, accent, and word division. Each dictionary has its own method for showing these things. On this dictionary page, where do you find the pronunciation of a word?
   a. It is placed in parentheses right after the word.
   b. It is indicated at the bottom of the page.
   c. It is placed at the end of each description.

   How does your own dictionary show pronunciation?

5. This dictionary page indicates accent by:
   a. using accent marks in the pronunciation guide.
   b. printing the accented syllable in bold type in the original word entry.
   c. printing the accented syllable in bold type in the pronunciation guide.

   How does your dictionary show accented syllables?

doggerel / Dominican

dogged is pronounced differently from the past form *dogged*.

dog·ger·el (daw-gĕ-rĕl) *n.* bad verse.

dog·gie, dog·gy (daw-gee) *n.* (*pl.* **dog·gies**) *(informal)* a dog. ☐**doggie** (or **doggy**) **bag**, a small bag provided by a restaurant for taking home uneaten food.

dog·gone (dawg-gawn) *adj.* *(informal)* pesky or annoying. ☐**doggone it**, *(informal)* damn it.

dog·house (dawg-hows) *n.* (*pl.* **-hous·es**, *pr.* -how-ziz) a dog's kennel. ☐**in the doghouse**, *(slang)* in disgrace.

do·gie (doh-gee) *n.* *(Western use)* a stray motherless calf.

dog·leg (dawg-leg) *n.* something bent at a sharp angle, especially a path or road.

dog·ma (dawg-mă) *n.* (*pl.* **-ma·ta**, *pr.* -mă-tă, **-mas**) a doctrine or doctrines put forward by some authority, especially a Church, to be accepted as true without question.

dog·ma·tic (dawg-mat-ik) *adj.* 1. of or like dogma. 2. putting forward statements in a firm authoritative way. **dog·mat′i·cal·ly** *adv.*

dog·ma·tism (dawg-mă-tiz-ĕm) *n.* being dogmatic.

dog·ma·tize (dawg-mă-tız) *v.* (**dog·ma·tized, dog·ma·tiz·ing**) to make dogmatic statements.

do-good·er (doo-guud-ĕr) *n.* a well-meaning but unrealistic reformer or philanthropist.

dog-tired (dawg-tırd) *adj.* tired out.

dog·tooth (dawg-tooth) *n.* a canine tooth. ☐**dogtooth violet**, a North American spring-flowering plant with yellow flowers having reddish spots.

dog·trot (dawg-trot) *n.* an easy steady trot like a dog's. **dogtrot** *v.* (**dog·trot·ted, dog·trot·ting**) to run this way.

dog·watch (dawg-woch) *n.* one of the two-hour watches on a ship (4–6 or 6–8 P.M.).

dog·wood (dawg-wuud) *n.* an American tree with small white or pink flowers and with bright red berries in the autumn.

Do·ha (doh-hah) the capital of Qatar.

doi·ly (doi-lee) *n.* (*pl.* **-lies**) a small ornamental mat placed under a dish or under cake etc. on a dish.

do·ings (doo-ingz) *n. pl.* things done or being done.

do-it-your·self (doo-it-yoor-self) *adj.* for use by an amateur. **do-it-yourself** *n.* **do-it-yourself′er** *n.*

dol. *abbr.* dollar(s).

dol·drums (dohl-drŭmz) *n. pl.* 1. the ocean regions near the equator where there is little or no wind. 2. a period of inactivity. ☐**in the doldrums**, in low spirits.

dole (dohl) *v.* (**doled, dol·ing**) to distribute sparingly, *dole it out.* **dole** *n.* *(informal)* a payment by a government to persons who are unable to find employment; *on the dole, (British)* receiving this.

dole·ful (dohl-fŭl) *adj.* mournful, sad. **dole′ful·ly** *adv.*

doll (dol) *n.* 1. a small model of a human figure, especially as a child's toy. 2. a pretty but empty-headed young woman. 3. *(slang)* a young woman, a lovable person. **doll** *v.* **doll up**, to dress smartly, *dolled herself up.*

dol·lar (dol-ăr) *n.* the unit of money in the U.S. and certain other countries. ☐**dollars and cents**, judged only in terms of the money involved.

dol·lop (dol-ŏp) *n.* a mass or quantity, a shapeless lump of something soft.

dol·ly (dol-ee) *n.* (*pl.* **-lies**) 1. *(informal)* a doll. 2. a movable platform for a heavy object.

dol·man (dohl-măn) **sleeve** a loose sleeve cut in one piece with the body of a garment.

dol·men (dohl-mĕn) *n.* a prehistoric structure with a large flat stone laid on upright ones.

do·lo·mite (doh-lŏ-mıt) *n.* a mineral or rock of calcium magnesium carbonate.

Do·lo·mites (doh-lŏ-mıts) *n. pl.* a rocky mountain range in north Italy.

do·lor·ous (doh-lŏ-rŭs) *adj.* mournful. **do′lor·ous·ly** *adv.* **do′lor·ous·ness** *n.*

dol·phin (dol-fin) *n.* 1. a sea animal like a porpoise but larger and with a beaklike snout. 2. either of two large fishes found in tropical waters and used as food.

dolt (dohlt) *n.* a stupid person.

dom. *abbr.* 1. domestic. 2. dominion.

-dom *suffix* used to form nouns with the meaning of rank, condition, or domain, as in *earldom, freedom, kingdom,* or group, as in *officialdom.*

do·main (doh-mayn) *n.* 1. a district or area under someone's control. 2. a field of thought or activity, *the domain of science.*

dome (dohm) *n.* 1. a rounded roof with a circular base. 2. something shaped like this.

domed (dohmd) *adj.* having a dome, shaped like a dome.

Domes·day (doomz-day) **Book** a record of the ownership of lands in England made in 1086 by order of William the Conqueror.

do·mes·tic (dŏ-mes-tik) *adj.* 1. of the home or household or family affairs. 2. of one's own country, not foreign or international, *domestic flights.* 3. (of animals) kept by man, not wild. **domestic** *n.* a servant in a household. **do·mes′ti·cal·ly** *adv.* ☐**domestic science**, the study of household management.

do·mes·ti·cate (dŏ-mes-ti-kayt) *v.* (**do·mes·ti·cat·ed, do·mes·ti·cat·ing**) 1. to become fond of home and its duties. 2. to tame (animals), to bring (animals) under control. **do·mes′ti·cat·ed** *adj.* **do·mes·ti·ca·tion** (dŏ-mes-ti-kay-shŏn) *n.*

do·mes·tic·i·ty (doh-mes-tis-i-tee) *n.* being domestic, domestic or home life.

dom·i·cile (dom-ĭ-sıl) *n.* a person's place of residence. **domicile** *v.* (**dom·i·ciled, dom·i·cil·ing**) to establish or settle in a place.

dom·i·ciled (dom-ĭ-sıld) *adj.* dwelling in a place.

dom·i·cil·i·ar·y (dom-ĭ-sil-i-er-ee) *adj.* of a dwelling place.

dom·i·nant (dom-i-nănt) *adj.* dominating. **dom′i·nance** *n.*

dom·i·nate (dom-i-nayt) *v.* (**dom·i·nat·ed, dom·i·nat·ing**) 1. to have a commanding influence over. 2. to be the most influential or conspicuous person or thing. 3. (of a high place) to tower over, *the mountain dominates the whole valley.* **dom·i·na·tion** (dom-i-nay-shŏn) *n.*

dom·i·neer (dom-i-neer) *v.* to behave in a forceful way, making others obey.

Dom·i·ni·ca (doh-mi-ni-că) an island country in the West Indies.

Do·min·i·can[1] (dŏ-min-i-kăn) *n.* a member of an order of friars founded by St. Dominic, or of a corresponding order of nuns. **Dominican** *adj.* of this order.

6. Circle the accented syllables in these words:

   (doi•lee)   (dohl•ful)   (do•mes•ti•kay•shon)   (dom•i•neer)

7. Words may have more than one meaning.
   a. How many meanings are given for **domestic**? (one—two—three)
   b. Which of the dictionary meanings is used here? "I like to drink **domestic** wine." (#1—#2—#3)
   c. Which of the dictionary meanings is used here? "The Smiths rarely have **domestic** problems." (#1—#2—#3)

8. a. How many meanings are given for **dominate**? (one—two—three)
   b. Write a sentence to illustrate meaning #1 of **dominate**.
      _____ .

9. Dictionaries show you the parts of speech of a word. Write the following forms:
   a. The adverb form of **domestic**: _____
   b. The plural noun of **doily**: _____
   c. The verb form of **domicile**: _____

10. In a dictionary, each major word is called an **entry**. Find:
    a. an entry for a suffix: _____
    b. the entry that is the informal word for **a dog**: _____
    c. the three entries related to "home and home life":
       1. _____   2. _____
       3. _____

11. Dictionary entries often include idioms associated with the entry word.
    a. What is the idiom listed under **doldrums**? (**dohl**-drumz—in the doldrums—a period of inactivity)
    b. Please find two other idiom entries on this page.
       1. _____   2. _____
    c. How are these idioms indicated? (by a number—by italics—by a □)
    d. In the entry **dominate**, is "the mountain dominates the whole valley" an idiom? If yes, why? If no, what is it?

G. **Word Forms:** Choose the correct word form to fit into each sentence referring to the chart as necessary. Use appropriate verb tenses, singular or plural forms for nouns, and passive voice where necessary.

Noun	Verb	Adjective	Adverb
choice	to choose	choice choosy	
educator education	to educate	educated educational	educationally
equality equal	to equal	equal	equally
interpreter interpretation	to interpret		
lawyer law	to legalize	legal	legally
leader leadership lead	to lead	leading	
marriage	to marry	marrying marriageable married	
progress progression	to progress	progressive	progressively
proof	to prove	proof	
responsibility		responsible	responsibly

1. **equality, equal, to equal, equal, equally**
   a. She is first among _____ .
   b. It is not always possible to divide the pie _____ .
   c. Is _____ more important than liberty?
   d. One tablespoon _____ three teaspoons.
   e. Do you support _____ rights for women?

2. **lawyer, law, to legalize, legal, legally**
   a. Dr. al-Awadhi is a _____ .
   b. She is a _____ professor at Kuwait University.
   c. Is this contract _____ ?
   d. Is it _____ binding over everyone who signed it?
   e. Do you think all drugs should be _____ ?

3. **interpreter, interpretation, to interpret**
   a. I don't understand your _____ of that passage.
   b. He is a bilingual _____ at the United Nations.
   c. Would you please _____ this passage for me?

4. **educator, education, to educate, educated, educational, educationally**
   a. Would you rather have a liberal arts or a vocational _____ ?
   b. She is a famous _____ .
   c. Traveling can certainly be _____ .
   d. What is the best way to _____ masses of people?
   e. Is this program _____ sound?
   f. She is a well-_____ person.

5. **progress, progression, to progress, progressive, progressively**
   a. He first became ill in March, and he got _____ worse after that.
   b. That school was considered quite _____ at one time.
   c. Tell me, do you see any _____ or are things still the same?
   d. He _____ slowly through the book and finished it in about three months.
   e. I don't see the logical _____ of these concepts, do you?

6. **proof, to prove, proof**
   a. This is 100-_____ vodka, so watch out!
   b. Where is the _____ for your argument?
   c. Can you _____ your statements?

7. **marriage, to marry, marrying, marriageable, married**
   a. They got _____ 15 years ago.
   b. Do you believe in _____ ?
   c. There are two _____ couples in this room, and the others are single.
   d. Is she of a _____ age? She looks very young.
   e. Besides, he's not the _____ kind.

8. **responsibility, responsible, responsibly**
   a. Don't avoid taking _____ .
   b. Of course, she is a very _____ worker.
   c. She handles her duties _____ .

9. **leader, leadership, lead, to lead, leading**
   a. He never did anything original; he always followed his partner's _____ .
   b. Do you think you would be a good _____ ?
   c. That is a _____ question if I ever heard one.
   d. You can _____ a horse to water, but you can't make it drink.
   e. What are the most important qualities in effective _____ ?

10. **choice, to choose, choice, choosy**

   a. He is impossible to please because he is so _____.

   b. Did you _____ to stay on longer or did you leave?

   c. What is your _____?

   d. That is a _____ bit of gossip if I ever heard one.

H. **Sentence Paraphrase: Make up new sentences using these sentence frames, and then make up your own sentences. You may add or leave out words, but try to retain the meaning of the original sentence.**

   Example: Dr. al-Awadhi said that she had not encountered resistance from her male colleagues.

      Dr. al-Awadhi said, "*I have not encountered resistance from my male colleagues.*"

      Other possible sentences: *Dr. al-Awadhi said that her male colleagues had not opposed her. According to Dr. al-Awadhi, her male colleagues had not opposed her.*

1. It was necessary for Dr. al-Awadhi to make sacrifices for her career.

   Dr. al-Awadhi _____

   sacrifices _____ career.

   Other possible sentences:

2. Dr. al-Awadhi's female students may not confront the same problems that she confronted because so many more women are being educated today.

   The problems _____ Dr. al-Awadhi

   _____ not _____ her female

   students because _____.

   Other possible sentences:

3. Distinguishing between Islamic law and Islamic custom, Dr. al-Awadhi points out that Islamic law supports the equality of women, but Islamic custom has not.

According to _____ , Islamic law _____
_____ , but Islamic

custom _____ .

Other possible sentences:

I. Topics for Discussion and Composition

1. The rewards of education are easy to name—personal enrichment, better job opportunities—but sometimes there are sacrifices that have to be made for education. Have you had to make any sacrifices for your education? What were they and why did you have to make them? Do you regret making these sacrifices? Why? Or why not?

2. Do you believe that women must make a choice between having a career and having a family? Why? Or why not? Give several specific reasons for your position and examples from your reading, your own experience, or the experience of others.

3. Career women can be as good mothers as women who stay home full-time. It is the quality of the mothering that counts, not the quantity. Do you agree or disagree? Why? Give several specific reasons for your position and examples from your reading, your own experience, or the experience of others.

4. Women cannot take pressure as well as men can, so they are not suited for leadership positions. Do you agree or disagree? Why? Or why not? Can you think of specific women in leadership positions who have demonstrated that they *can* take pressure? If so, who are these women, what were the situations, and how did they react?

5. Name three women in the history of the world whom you admire. Why do you admire each of these women? What have you learned from their lives?

6. Do you think women have to pay a price for professional success? Is the price greater than the price paid by men? Why? Or why not? Give examples to illustrate your position.

J. **Reading Reconstruction: Read this paragraph as many times as you can in three minutes. Then, with your book closed, try to restate the ideas in writing as clearly and completely as you can. (See exercise J in Chapter 1 for complete instructions.)**

Changing Times

Just a few years ago, women like Dr. al-Awadhi had to choose between a higher education and having a family. Naturally this was a very difficult choice. But now, many young men in countries like Kuwait want to marry educated women, and it is no disadvantage to a woman to be educated. Her marriage prospects may, in fact, be improved. However, she still may not be able to have a career after her marriage, particularly after children are born. This custom may change too before long as more and more educated women marry and have families. Women may demand to have careers. Also, developing countries may want to encourage all educated people, men and women, to contribute to the workforce. These countries may regard educated women as a rich natural resource.

Key words (to be written on the chalkboard):

Dr. al-Awadhi	prospects	developing countries
choose	improved	encourage
higher education	custom	contribute
family	women	workforce
difficult	demand	natural
no disadvantage	careers	resource
marriage		

Comprehension Check

On a separate piece of paper, write the numbers 1 through 10 on both sides. Mark one side "Test 1" and the other side "Test 2." Read each statement and decide whether it is true or false. Write "T" after true statements and "F" after false statements under Test 1. After you have finished the comprehension check, turn Test 1 face down. Then read the article again and do the comprehension check again under Test 2. Base your answers on the information in this article *only*, even if you disagree with what the author said.

1. Islamic law supports the equality of women.

2. According to Dr. al-Awadhi, the problem for women has been connected with the interpretation of Islamic law, not Islamic law itself.

3. Islamic law forbids the education of women.

4. Islamic law is usually interpreted by women.

5. More than half of the lawyers in Kuwait are now women.

6. Women are not allowed to attend the university in Kuwait.

7. Dr. al-Awadhi is a typical Kuwaiti woman.

8. Dr. al-Awadhi had to choose between a family and a career.

9. Young Kuwaiti women students may not face the same problems that Dr. al-Awadhi had to face.

10. Dr. al-Awadhi was a member of parliament at the time the article was written.

3

Before you read, here are some questions to think about:

— Do you ever have trouble falling asleep? Do you wake up in the middle of the night and find yourself unable to fall asleep again?

— How do you feel when you haven't had enough sleep?

— How much sleep do you think adults need? How much sleep do *you* need?

— What do you do when you can't fall asleep? Does it help?

HOW TO COPE WITH INSOMNIA

[Millions of people are plagued by difficulty in falling asleep—and staying asleep. Here are some medically proven ways to get a better night's sleep without dangerous or habit-forming drugs.]

1   Many of us still believe that in order to be healthy we must have eight hours of sleep a night; or that if we sleep poorly over a period of time, we'll get lines in our faces, bags under our eyes, a worn look, and worst of all, be unable to perform our daily tasks efficiently.

2   "Untrue," says Dr. Alice Kuhn Schwartz, psychologist and co-author of *Somniquest.* "You may look awful to *yourself,* but except for the first hour or so in the morning when you probably will be puffy-eyed due to depletion of a certain hormone that's the result of lack of sleep, you'll soon look like your usual self and perform normally. If you do feel worn, the cause is stress, not lack of sleep. Also, there is no set number of hours you must sleep to maintain good health. Some people get along beautifully on four and a half hours, others sleep nine hours. Anywhere within that range is normal."

What causes insomnia?

3   Recent studies of patients at sleep clinics have revealed significant facts about the causes of insomnia as well as ways to deal with it. It's no surprise that stress and depression (over family, health, job, or other problems) are linked to insomnia. Also, insomnia may be caused by physical illness: itching, aches, asthma, arthritis, ulcers, and heart problems that involve shortness of breath or difficulty in breathing.

4   In order to overcome insomnia, millions of Americans turn to drugs—both over-the-counter drugs and prescription drugs. "No pill will produce normal sleep," says Dr. James Minard, sponsor of Sleep Studies at New Jersey Medical School. "You reach no proper levels of sleep through a pill; you're merely sedated."

How can you cure it?

5   What can you do if you suffer from insomnia? Two things: you can eat certain foods that will help you fall asleep and stay asleep, and you can do certain things that are sleep-inducing. Here are some guidelines Dr. Schwartz has worked out after years of research.

a. If you've had a bad night's sleep, don't stay in bed later the next morning.

b. Don't go to bed earlier the next night. Stick to your usual bedtime and rising pattern.

c. Don't nap during the day. Naps cut down on night sleep-time.

d. Never lie awake in bed for more than 30 minutes. By lying in bed sleepless you form an association between your bed and sleeplessness, thus reinforcing your poor sleeping pattern.

e. When you get out of bed after half an hour of sleeplessness, do something, but make sure it's something dull. Read a book that doesn't interest you much. Never watch TV or listen to the radio.

f. Try sitting still in a chair in a darkened room; you'll be surprised how fast you'll get sleepy.

g. When you retire for the night, don't lie there rehashing the mistakes of the day. Nor is this the time to plan your next day's activities—you may become too anxious or overstimulated.

h. Get as much exercise as possible, preferably early in the day. Exercise is a great sleep inducer.

i. Develop a bedtime routine: closing up the house and turning out the lights in a certain way, bathing, plumping up the pillows. Sleep studies show that doing things in sequence—in a way that tends to calm and soothe—can help you achieve a good sleep pattern.

6   As for food intake to help you sleep, make sure that your daily diet is a balanced one and high in tryptophan, an amino acid found in certain foods. The body converts tryptophan to L-tryptophan and then to serotonin, a body chemical crucial to the sleep process. Foods rich in tryptophan are: whole or skim milk, eggs, cheese, meat, cashews and peanuts, apples, bananas, cherries, figs, dried prunes, and watermelon. If you include foods high in tryptophan in your daily diet, and incorporate some of the sleep-inducing activities into your life, the chances are good that you will achieve a pattern of restful, soothing sleep.

TURN TO COMPREHENSION CHECK AT END OF CHAPTER

660 words

READING TIMES:
1st reading _____ minutes
2nd reading _____ minutes

READING SPEED:
6 minutes = 110 wpm
5 minutes = 132 wpm
4 minutes = 166 wpm
3 minutes = 221 wpm

A. **Analysis of Ideas and Relationships: Circle the letter next to the best answer.**

1. The main idea of this article is that:
   a. insomnia is a common problem, but there are no cures for it.
   b. there are ways to cope with insomnia.
   c. people with insomnia tend to be unhealthy.

   Please explain your answer.

2. Paragraph 2 explains:
   a. why the statements in paragraph 1 are untrue.
   b. why you should sleep 8 hours every night.
   c. why you look awful to yourself.

3. Paragraph 3 gives examples of:
   a. recent studies at sleep clinics.
   b. ways to deal with insomnia.
   c. some causes of insomnia.

4. Read paragraph 4. If a person with a sleep problem came to Dr. Minard, he would:
   a. probably not recommend a sleeping pill.
   b. definitely recommend a sleeping pill.
   c. have the person sedated.

   Why did you choose your answer?

5. Look over the list of guidelines in paragraph 5. Which of the following would Dr. Schwartz probably approve of doing if you can't sleep? Circle all that apply.
   a. Read an exciting novel.
   b. Go to bed at your usual bedtime.
   c. Go swimming in the morning.
   d. Think about a meeting you have to attend tomorrow.
   e. Take a nap at lunchtime.

   Please explain your answers.

6. In paragraph 5, item e, Dr. Schwartz implies, **but does not directly say,** that:
   a. you should read a book that doesn't interest you much.
   b. watching TV or reading an interesting book will stimulate you and keep you awake.
   c. listening to the radio will wake up other people in your house.

7. Sleep studies show that doing things _____A_____ can help you _____B_____ a good sleep pattern. (Choose one word from Group A and one word from Group B.)
   A: at random—by yourself—in sequence—on time
   B: achieve—lose—turn out—fall asleep

8. The third sentence in paragraph 6 is a list of foods. Paragraph 6:
   a. does not explain why these foods are listed here.
   b. says to avoid the foods listed.
   c. highly recommends that you eat the foods listed.

9. The last sentence of paragraph 6:
   a. is pessimistic about insomnia.
   b. contains examples of food high in tryptophan.
   c. summarizes the entire article.

   Please explain.

10. A good title for this article would be:
    a. I Want to Go to Sleep.
    b. Causes of Insomnia and Ways to Deal with It.
    c. Foods to Help You Sleep.

B. Interpretation of Words and Phrases: Circle the letter next to the best answer.

1. In paragraph 1 ("Many of us still believe . . ."), **still** means:
   a. even now.
   b. quietly.
   c. carefully.

2. **Worst of all,** we'll be unable to perform our daily tasks efficiently.
   a. The best one can say is that
   b. The most unpleasant aspect is that
   c. Regardless of what else we might want to do with our time,

3. **Except for** the first hour or so, you'll look like your usual self.
   a. During
   b. For approximately
   c. Other than

4. "If you do feel **worn,** the cause is stress...."
   a. tired
   b. old
   c. like wearing old clothes

5. Millions of Americans **turn to** drugs to overcome insomnia.
   a. refuse to use
   b. decide to use
   c. open bottles of

6. "**Stick to** your usual bedtime and rising pattern."
   a. Keep on using
   b. Change
   c. Add something to

7. In paragraph 5, sentence f ("Try sitting still in a chair..."), **still** means:
   a. even now.
   b. quietly.
   c. carefully.

8. "**Make sure** your daily diet is a balanced one...."
   a. Prepare fresh foods so
   b. Don't worry whether
   c. Be careful to ensure that

9. In paragraph 6, what is **tryptophan?**
   a. An amino acid that is converted to serotonin.
   b. An amino acid that is balanced.
   c. An amino acid found in all foods.

10. "**The chances are good that** you will achieve a pattern of restful, soothing sleep."
    a. It is unclear whether
    b. It is definite that
    c. It is quite probable that

C. **Synonyms: From this list, choose a synonym for the word in bold type in each sentence. Use appropriate tenses for verbs and singular or plural forms for nouns.**

to calm	the inability to sleep	specific
connected	in the specific order	to strengthen
helpful suggestion	only	to take in
important		

1. You do not need to sleep a **set** number of hours.

2. Exercise is one of the best cures for **insomnia.**

3. The report told all the **significant** facts about insomnia.

4. Depression and stress are **linked** to insomnia.

5. If you take sleeping pills, you are **merely** sedated.

6. Here are some **guidelines** for overcoming insomnia.

7. Try **to reinforce** your good sleeping habits.

8. Be sure to follow the directions **in sequence,** or else you'll have trouble!

9. A hot bath **soothes** and relaxes me before I go to sleep.

10. The report **incorporates** many ideas about sleep.

D. **Prepositions and Verb-Completers: Write any appropriate preposition or verb-completer in the blank spaces.**

1. _____ order _____ be healthy, we must have eight hours _____ sleep.

2. If we sleep poorly, we'll get lines _____ our faces and bags _____ our eyes.

3. Except _____ the first hour or so _____ the morning, you'll look like your usual self.

4. Anywhere _____ that range is normal.

5. Recent studies have revealed significant facts _____ the causes _____ insomnia as well as ways _____ deal _____ it.

6. What can you do if you suffer _____ insomnia?

7. _____ lying _____ bed sleepless, you form an association _____ your bed and sleeplessness.

8. When you get _____ _____ bed, do something dull.

9. Doing things _____ a way that tends _____ calm and soothe can help you achieve a good sleep pattern.

10. Incorporate some _____ the sleep-inducing activities _____ your life.

E. **Special Expressions: These special expressions are all related to the topic of sleep. In the following sentences, fill in each space with an appropriate expression.**

to go to bed	asleep—sleeping	to be awakened by
to fall asleep	awake	to get up—to rise
to stay in bed	to lie awake	to sleep late
to sleep	to wake up	to take a nap—to nap
sleepy	to wake (someone) up	bedtime

1. My brother usually _____ at 6:30 A.M., and _____ immediately.

2. Last night he _____ at 11:30 P.M., but couldn't _____ until past 1 A.M. He _____ for a long time thinking about some problems.

3. Since tomorrow is a holiday, I can _____ . (I don't have to get up early.)

4. My children always _____ me _____ early on Sunday mornings.

5. People generally _____ about eight hours a night.

6. Yesterday I _____ a loud noise outside my window at 5 A.M.

7. Young children often become _____ in the afternoon, and their mothers make them _____ .

8. Last night I couldn't sleep. I went to bed at my usual _____ , but I stayed _____ almost all night.

9. When I was sick, the doctor told me to _____ and rest.

F.   Multiple-Word Verbs: From this list, choose a synonym for each multiple-word verb in bold type in the sentences. Be sure to use an appropriate verb tense for each sentence. Some synonyms may be used more than once.

to convert . . . into	to develop	to leave
to decrease	to handle	to manage
to deplete	to induce	to perform

1. What do you do **to cope with** insomnia?

2. Some people **get along** on four and a half hour's sleep.

3. When a certain hormone **is used up,** you will probably become puffy-eyed.

4. Recent studies have revealed ways **to deal with** insomnia.

5. There are certain things you can do **to bring on** sleep.

6. Dr. Schwartz **has worked out** some guidelines.

7. Naps **cut down on** sleep-time.

8. What time do you **get out of** work?

9. Do you have any difficulty **carrying out** your job if you haven't slept well?

10. The body **turns** tryptophan **into** L-tryptophan.

G.   Word Forms: Choose the correct word form to fit into each sentence. Use appropriate verb tenses, singular or plural forms for nouns, and passive voice where necessary.

Noun	*Verb*	*Adjective*	*Adverb*
achievement achiever	to achieve	achievable	
anxiety		anxious	anxiously
belief	to believe	believable unbelievable	unbelievably
breath	to breathe	breathless	breathlessly
conversion convert	to convert	convertible	
cure	to cure	curable incurable	incurably

Noun	Verb	Adjective	Adverb
depletion	to deplete		
form	to form	formative ·	
formation			
probability		probable	probably
producer	to produce	productive	productively
product			
production			
productively			

1. **belief, to believe, believable, unbelievable, unbelievably**
   a. It's almost _____ what modern medicine can do!
   b. Although no one thought his story was _____ , I believed him.
   c. The Hawaiian Islands are _____ beautiful.
   d. Many people _____ that you need eight hours of sleep every night.
   e. Do you share this _____ ?

2. **probability, probable, probably**
   a. What is the _____ that your parents will visit the U.S. next year?
   b. They will _____ come in May or June.
   c. It is _____ that we will take them on a tour of New England.

3. **depletion, to deplete**
   a. It's important for a nation not to _____ its energy resources.
   b. A _____ of Vitamin C can cause gum and tooth disease.

4. **breath, to breathe, breathless, breathlessly**
   a. Whenever my brother exercises too hard, he gets out of _____ .
   b. It is so hot in here that I can hardly _____ .
   c. By the time we climbed up the fifth flight of stairs, we were _____ .
   d. After he had been running, he spoke _____ .

5. **producer, product, production, productivity, to produce, productive, productively**
   a. _____ in this factory will definitely increase with the use of these new machines.
   b. What kinds of _____ does your company make?
   c. Our company _____ soaps and other cleaning agents.
   d. The company had its most _____ year in 1983.
   e. Mr. Jensen spent his weekend _____ and finished everything he had to do.
   f. Have you seen the recent _____ of "My Fair Lady"?
   g. Who is the _____ of the play?

6. **cure, to cure, curable, incurable, incurably**
   a. Martin's father has an _____ disease. There is no known treatment.
   b. What is your favorite _____ for a sore throat?
   c. Pneumonia can _____ by treatments of antibiotics.
   d. Some forms of cancer are now _____ if they are discovered early.
   e. He is _____ ill.

7. **form, formation, to form, formative**
   a. Please fill out these three _____ and leave them on my desk.
   b. The _____ of good sleeping habits will help cure your insomnia.
   c. The project is only in its _____ stage, but it should be developed by next month.
   d. I _____ many lasting friendships when I was in college.

8. **anxiety, anxious, anxiously**
   a. The whole class waited _____ for the results of the examination.
   b. After hearing the bad news, Mr. Dumont was _____ to get home.
   c. It was a difficult decision, and she felt some _____ making it.

9. **achievement, achiever, to achieve, achievable**
   a. That was a great _____ ! I am proud of you.
   b. The brilliant scientist _____ great success in her life.
   c. There was a time when people doubted that space flight was _____ .
   d. Over-_____ always try to be the best at whatever they do.

10. **conversion, convert, to convert, convertible**
    a. The president has made many _____ to his point of view from among the senators.
    b. Quite a few senators _____ to his philosophy already.
    c. _____ to the metric system will not be easy in the United States.
    d. My favorite kind of car has a _____ top.

H. Sentence Construction: Use each group of words in the order and form given to construct an original, meaningful sentence. Various sentences can be made from each group of words.

1. surprise, stress, depression, linked to, insomnia

2. pill, produce, sleep

3. guidelines, worked out, years, research

4. studies, show, in sequence, achieve, pattern

5. make sure, diet, balanced, tryptophan

I. Topics for Discussion and Composition

1. When people have insomnia, they cannot function normally. What are some of the bad effects on people who have had too little sleep? What happens to their senses, reactions, and emotions? Give several examples to explain your answer.

2. This article mentions that people take various drugs that artificially cause them to fall asleep. Do you think people should take drugs to make them fall asleep, to wake up easily, or to change their personality? Why or why not? Give several examples to support your answer.

3. Paragraph 5 offers some guidelines to help you fall asleep. Do you know of other methods that could help a person fall asleep? Do you have a favorite method of your own?

4. Paragraph 6 mentions some foods that should help you sleep. In the United States, a traditional way to become sleepy is to drink hot milk before going to bed. Are there any foods that people in your country like to eat or drink at bedtime? How are these foods supposed to help people fall asleep? Are these foods related to those on the list in paragraph 6?

J. Reading Reconstruction: Read this paragraph as many times as you can in three minutes. Then, with your book closed, try to restate the ideas in writing as clearly and completely as you can. (See exercise J in Chapter 1 for complete instructions.)

Sleep Research Today

Although sleep research has improved our understanding of sleep and insomnia, researchers still do not know just why sleep is necessary. Sleep doesn't seem to be essential for health since some people can get along with very little sleep. Nor does sleep merely give us back energy that was depleted during the day. Some of the most significant new studies link sleep to our "body clock," where certain patterns occur in sequence.

Some researchers believe that during sleep the brain and nervous system carry out necessary activities. People with insomnia are often anxious or depressed. They can often cope with their troubled thoughts during the day, but as they try to fall asleep, their bodies relax. Then it becomes impossible to avoid these thoughts. This reinforces their insomnia. The chances are they will need medical help to cure their sleeplessness.

Key words (to be written on the chalkboard):

sleep	"body clock"	people	thoughts
research	brain	insomnia	reinforces
not essential	nervous system	anxious	medical help
health	necessary activities	depressed	cure

Comprehension Check

On a separate piece of paper, write the numbers 1 through 10 on both sides. Mark one side "Test 1" and the other side "Test 2." Read each statement and decide whether it is true or false. Write "T" after true statements and "F" after false statements under Test 1. After you have finished the comprehension check, turn Test 1 face down. Then read the article again and do the comprehension check again under Test 2. Base your answers on the information in this article *only*, even if you disagree with what the author said.

1. It is necessary for all adults to sleep eight hours a night.

2. Some people can get along on four and a half hours of sleep.

3. Researchers are now studying the causes of insomnia and ways to deal with it.

4. Sleeping pills can help you sleep normally.

5. Stress, depression, and physical illness may all cause insomnia.

6. Dr. Schwartz advises that you stay in bed even if you can't sleep.

7. It's a good idea to read a dull book if you can't sleep.

8. Tryptophan is an amino acid found in all foods.

9. Milk and eggs are rich in tryptophan.

10. If you eat foods rich in tryptophan and include some sleep-inducing activities in your life, you will probably be able to sleep well.

4

Before you read, here are some questions to think about:

— What are some of the differences between human and non-human intelligence?

— Are humans the only animals that can use language?

— Have you ever heard of other animals (non-humans) learning to use language? If so, please explain.

— What does it mean to be able to use language?

CONVERSATIONS WITH A GORILLA

[This article describes Koko, a remarkable language-using gorilla. Using sign language, she has a vocabulary of at least 375 words which she uses regularly and accurately. Her trainer, Dr. Francine Patterson, is a researcher in language and communication. She became involved with Koko when the gorilla was nine months old.]

1   Koko is a seven-year-old "talking" gorilla. She is the focus of my career as a developmental psychologist, and also has become a dear friend. Through mastery of sign language—the familiar hand speech of the deaf—Koko has made us, her human companions, aware not only that her breed is bright, but also that it shares sensitivities commonly held to be the prerogative of people.

2   Take Koko's touching empathy toward fellow animals. Seeing a horse with a bit in its mouth, she signed, "Horse sad." When asked why the horse was sad, she signed, "Teeth." Shown a photo of the famous albino gorilla Snowflake struggling against having a bath, Koko, who also hates baths, signed, "Me cry there," while pointing at the picture. But Koko responds to more complicated motivations, too. She loves an argument and is not averse to trading insults.

3   What makes all this awesome—even for me, after six years of witnessing such incidents—is that Koko, by all accepted concepts of animal and human nature, should not be able to do any of this. Traditionally, such behavior has been considered uniquely human; yet here is a language-using gorilla.

4   On our first meeting, Koko did nothing to advance the cause of gorilla public relations. Quickly sizing me up, the tiny 20-pound gorilla bit me on the leg. But I was undeterred. People often ask if I am worried about dealing with Koko when she reaches full growth, perhaps 250 pounds. The answer is no, though at 130 pounds she already outweighs me and is astonishingly strong. While many captive chimpanzees become difficult to work with as they mature, gorillas seem to be of quite a different temperament.

5   Vocabulary development is one of the best indexes of human intelligence. Koko's vocabulary grew at a remarkable pace. Over the first year and a half, she acquired about one new sign every month. By six and a half, she had used 645 different signs. Finally, I would estimate that Koko's current working vocabulary—signs she uses regularly and appropriately—stands at about 375.

6   From the start, I monitored Koko's performance on human intelligence tests. Testing Koko's IQ has not been easy. There is, for instance, a cultural bias toward humans that shows up when tests are administered to a gorilla. One quiz asked the child, "Point to the two things that are good to eat." The depicted objects were a block, an apple, a shoe, a flower, and an ice cream sundae. Koko, reflecting her gorilla tastes, picked the apple and the flower. Another asked the child to pick where he would run to shelter from the rain. The choices were a hat, a spoon, a tree, and a house. Koko naturally chose the tree. Rules for the scoring required that I record these responses as errors.

7   Evidence I have been accumulating strongly suggests that Koko expresses a make-believe capacity similar to humans'. At about the age of five, Koko discovered the value of the lie to get herself out of a jam. After numerous repeat performances I'm convinced that Koko is really lying in these circumstances and not merely making mistakes. One of her first lies also involved the reconstruction of an earlier happening. My assistant Kate Mann was with Koko, then tipping the scales at 90 pounds, when the gorilla plumped down on the kitchen sink in the trailer and it separated from its frame and dropped out of alignment. Later, when I asked Koko if she broke the sink, she signed, "Kate there bad," pointing to the sink. Koko couldn't know, of course, that I would never accept the idea that Kate would go around breaking sinks.

8   Koko is defining objects. "What is a stove?" I ask her. She points to the stove. "What do you do with it?" "Cook with." "What is an orange?" "Food, drink."

9   She perceives right and wrong, but is touchy about blame. During a videotaping session, when I turn away, she tries to steal grapes from a bowl. I scold her. "Stop stealing. Don't be such a pig. Be polite. Ask me. Stealing is wrong, wrong, like biting and hurting are wrong." Then I ask, "What does Penny do that's wrong?" Koko says, "Break things, lie, tell me 'polite' [when I'm] hungry pig."

10   Finally, Koko is learning self-esteem. A reporter asks about Koko as a person. I turn to Koko: "Are you an animal or a person?"

11   Koko's instant response: "Fine animal gorilla."

TURN TO COMPREHENSION CHECK AT END OF CHAPTER

737 words

READING TIMES:
1st reading _____ minutes
2nd reading _____ minutes

READING SPEED:
7 minutes = 105 wpm
6 minutes = 123 wpm
5 minutes = 147 wpm
4 minutes = 184 wpm
3 minutes = 246 wpm

A. **Analysis of Ideas and Relationships: Circle the letter next to the best answer.**

1. In paragraphs 1 and 2, Dr. Patterson implies **but does not directly say,** that:
   a. gorillas are smarter than people.
   b. Koko is a seven-year-old, 130-pound talking gorilla.
   c. humans are not the only living creatures to have emotions.

2. In sentence 3 of paragraph 1, the phrase "... the familiar hand speech of the deaf..." is between two dashes (—):
   a. to emphasize the definition of sign language.
   b. to emphasize why deaf people use sign language.
   c. to emphasize how difficult it is to learn sign language.

3. In paragraph 2, when Koko said, "Horse sad," she meant that:
   a. the horse must be sad because it had a bit in its mouth.
   b. the horse must be sad because it didn't have any teeth.
   c. all horses are sad.

4. In paragraph 4, "... the tiny 20-pound gorilla bit me on the leg" is an explanation that clarifies the sentence:
   a. "But I was undeterred."
   b. "On our first meeting, Koko did nothing to advance the cause of gorilla public relations."
   c. "People often ask if I am worried about dealing with Koko when she reaches full growth ..."

5. In paragraph 6, sentence 6 ("Koko, reflecting ....") shows an example of:
   a. a gorilla's intelligence.
   b. cultural bias.
   c. both a and b.

Please explain your answer.

6. In paragraph 6, the last sentence ("Rules for the scoring required that I record these responses as errors.") means that:
   a. Koko didn't understand the questions and just guessed at the answers.
   b. although Koko answered correctly *for a gorilla,* the only correct answers were the ones that a human child would give.
   c. gorillas and children give the same responses, but the answers given by a gorilla would be counted as errors.

7. Paragraph 6 discusses in general:
   a. the difficulty of giving an IQ test to a non-human.
   b. Koko's new words in sign language.
   c. aspects of Koko's personality.

8. In paragraph 7, what does the story about Kate and the sink tell you about Koko's personality?
   a. Koko knows how to lie.
   b. Koko doesn't understand what happened to the sink.
   c. Koko weighs 90 pounds.

9. The title of this article refers to:
   a. Koko's ability to speak with her trainers.
   b. how Koko communicates with sign language.
   c. a lecture that the trainer gave about Koko.

10. If you were to ask Koko's trainer about her future research, she would probably say that:
   a. Koko has learned all she can and will be sent back to a zoo soon.
   b. she wants to continue doing much more research with gorillas.
   c. gorillas are much smarter than chimpanzees.

   Why did you choose your answer?

B. Interpretation of Words and Phrases: Circle the letter next to the best answer.

1. "Koko has made **us, her** human companions, aware not only that her breed is bright, but also that **it** shares sensitivities commonly held to be the prerogative of people."

us refers to:	**her** refers to:	**it** refers to:
a. breed	a. breed	a. breed
b. Koko	b. Koko	b. Koko
c. the trainers	c. the trainers	c. the trainers

2. Koko loves to **trade insults.**
   a. go to the store.
   b. argue back and forth with her trainers.
   c. have her trainers tell her she is bad.

3. "Koko, **by all accepted concepts of animal and human nature**, should not be able to do any of this."
   a. based on anything we know about animals and humans
   b. acting as a good example of animals and humans
   c. believing that she is a human and not an animal

4. "Quickly **sizing me up**, the tiny 20-pound gorilla bit me on the leg."
   a. measuring my height
   b. deciding she didn't like me
   c. understanding the type of person I was

5. "By six and a half, she had used 645 different signs." **Six and a half** refers to:
   a. the number of months it took to learn 645 signs.
   b. six and a half years of training.
   c. Koko's age.

6. "Koko expresses a make-believe capacity similar to humans'." **Humans'** has an apostrophe (') because:
   a. it is a plural possessive word and refers to humans' make-believe capacity.
   b. the author is surprised that Koko has a make-believe capacity.
   c. it indicates that Koko is similar to a human being.

7. "Koko expresses a **make-believe** capacity similar to humans'."
   a. imaginative
   b. realistic
   c. valuable

8. Koko knows how to lie her way out of **a jam**.
   a. a crowded place.
   b. a difficult situation.
   c. a meal with sweet food.

9. "... the gorilla plumped down on the kitchen sink and **it** separated from its frame." **It** refers to:
   a. Koko.
   b. the frame.
   c. the sink.

10. "Koko is touchy about blame."
    a. Koko likes to touch people.
    b. Koko likes to blame others for her mistakes.
    c. Koko is very sensitive about being blamed for her mistakes.

C. **Synonyms:** From this list choose a synonym for the word in bold type in each sentence. Be sure to use correct verb tenses and singular or plural forms for nouns.

to accuse	to grow older	to see
astonishing	opposed	special power
capability	persistent	to write down
to gather		

1. These sensitivities are commonly held to be the **prerogative** of people.

2. Koko is not **averse** to trading insults.

3. Don't you think Koko's accomplishments are **awesome**?

4. The trainers **witnessed** many incidents of Koko's ability.

5. The trainer is **undeterred** in her efforts to teach sign language to Koko.

6. Chimpanzees become difficult to work with as they **mature**.

7. She **records** Koko's scores on the IQ tests.

8. Evidence I have been **accumulating** suggests that Koko knows how to lie.

9. Koko has a make-believe **capacity** similar to humans'.

10. Koko signed, "Don't **blame** me. I didn't do it!"

D. **Prepositions and Verb-Completers:** Write any appropriate preposition or verb-completer in the blank spaces.

1. Koko is the focus _____ my career.

2. She saw a horse _____ a bit _____ its mouth.

3. Koko should not be able _____ do any _____ this.

4. People ask me if I am worried _____ dealing _____ a 250-pound gorilla.

5. Vocabulary development is one _____ the best indexes _____ human intelligence.

6. _____ the start, I have monitored Koko's performance _____ human intelligence tests.

7. _____ about age five, she discovered the value _____ a lie.

8. Koko will lie her way _____ _____ a jam.

9. Koko plumped down _____ the kitchen sink and it separated _____ its frame.

10. "What do you do _____ a stove?"

E. **Dictionary Skills: All the words in bold type have several different meanings. Look up each word in your dictionary and decide which is the correct meaning for the word *as it is used in the paragraph.***

1. This **article** describes Koko, a remarkable language-using gorilla.
   a. **article:**   "a, an" — short written piece — clause in a contract

2. Koko is a seven-year-old "talking" gorilla. She is the **focus** of my career as a developmental psychologist, and also has become a **dear** friend. Through mastery of sign language—the familiar hand speech of the deaf—Koko has made us, her human companions, aware not only that her breed is **bright**, but also that it shares sensitivities **commonly** held to be the prerogative of people.
   a. **focus:**   central point — to make clear — geometric term
   b. **dear:**   expensive — cherished — opening word in a letter
   c. **bright:**   clever — well lit — colorful
   d. **commonly:**   generally — publicly — below standard

3. Take Koko's **touching** empathy toward **fellow** animals. Seeing a horse with a **bit** in its mouth, she signed, "Horse sad." When asked why the horse was sad, she signed, "Teeth." She loves an argument and is not averse to **trading** insults.
   a. **touching:**   bodily contact — compassionate — comparing
   b. **fellow:**   man — a member of a society — equivalent
   c. **bit:**   a very small piece — ate — part of a horse's bridle
   d. **trading:**   business — exchanging — negotiating

F. Special Expressions: Here are some words that express likes, dislikes, and emotions. Choose the correct synonym for each word in bold type. Be sure to use correct verb tenses and singular or plural forms for nouns.

beloved   to say something that is not true
easily offended   self-respect
emotional capacity   sympathy
personality   uncomplimentary remark
to reprimand

1. Koko has become my **dear** friend.

2. Koko shares **sensitivities** with humans.

3. Koko shows **empathy** for her fellow animals.

4. The angry men said terrible **insults** to each other.

5. Gorillas and chimpanzees seem to be of a different **temperament.**

6. My parents taught me that it is wrong **to lie**.

7. Don't be so **touchy!** I was only joking.

8. The trainer **scolded** Koko when Koko tried to steal grapes.

9. Even a gorilla shows some **self-esteem**.

G. **Word Forms:** Choose the correct word form to fit into each sentence referring to the chart as necessary. Use appropriate verb tenses, singular or plural forms for nouns, and passive voice where necessary.

Noun	Verb	Adjective	Adverb
acceptance	to accept	acceptable accepted	
administration administrator	to administer	administrative	administratively
argument	to argue	argumentative	
deterrent	to deter	undeterred	
incidence incident		incidental	incidentally
instance		instant instantaneous	instantly
intelligence		intelligent	intelligently
involvement	to involve	involved	
perception	to perceive	perceptive	perceptively
sensitivity sensation sense	to sense	sensitive	sensitively

1. **sensitivity, sensation, sense, to sense, sensitive, sensitively**
   a. Use common _____ to figure out that problem.
   b. After the accident, Peter lost all _____ in his left leg.
   c. If you have a _____ to dust, you must keep your apartment very clean.
   d. Joanna is very _____ about her height, so don't ask her how tall she is.
   e. As soon as I walked into the room, I _____ something was wrong.
   f. Doctors should speak _____ to their patients.

2. **argument, to argue, argumentative**
   a. Listen to the Smiths. They _____ so loudly now!
   b. People who are very _____ rarely have many friends.
   c. Let's promise not to have any more _____ .

3. **incidence, incident, incidental, incidentally**
   a. I saw the big fire. It was just _____ that I was there when it happened.
   b. The newspaper described the _____ in a front page story.
   c. _____ , did you know there was a fire in my neighborhood, too?
   d. The _____ of fires increases in the winter because people are careless with their heaters.

4. **deterrent, to deter, undeterred**
   a. What is the best _____ to crime?
   b. The thief _____ by the barking dog.
   c. No matter what you say, I will remain _____ !

5. **intelligence, intelligent, intelligently**
   a. _____ people should use their abilities to the greatest possible extent.
   b. The economist wrote very _____ about the problems of unemployment.
   c. Koko shows true _____ in her ability to use signs.

6. **instance, instant, instantaneous, instantly**
   a. In this _____ , I think you are wrong.
   b. The change was _____ after the doctor gave him the injection.
   c. Milton realized _____ that he had said the wrong thing, so he apologized.
   d. Her _____ reply was, "Yes, I will marry you."

7. **administration, administrator, to administer, administrative, administratively**
   a. Mr. Dong is the top _____ in the company.
   b. He _____ all aspects of the company's finances.
   c. _____ the company is divided into three units.
   d. The _____ officers all work on the 10th floor.
   e. The university _____ is located in the tall building over there.

8. **involvement, to involve, involved**
   a. Don't _____ me in your personal problems.
   b. Those results are based on very _____ calculations.
   c. My _____ with animals resulted in my becoming a veterinarian.

9. **acceptance, to accept, acceptable, accepted**
   a. Her excuse _____ by her teacher.
   b. It is an _____ fact that exercise is good for your health.
   c. It will be _____ for you to come by 8 P.M., but not later.
   d. In her speech of _____ , the new mayor thanked her campaign manager and all the volunteers.

10. **perception, to perceive, perceptive, perceptively**
    a. Mr. Sherman _____ by everyone as being very competent.
    b. Tolstoy and Shakespeare wrote _____ on the human condition.
    c. I am surprised that Koko has a _____ of right and wrong.
    d. A doctor needs to be _____ when she questions a patient.

H. Sentence Construction: Use each group of words in the given order and form to make an original, meaningful sentence.

1. Koko, made us aware, bright, shares, sensitivities

2. gorillas, seem, different temperament, chimpanzees

3. vocabulary development, best indexes, intelligence

4. testing, IQ, easy

5. Koko, make-believe, similar, humans'

I. Topics for Discussion and Composition

1. Have you ever seen gorillas or other animals that seemed to be intelligent? Explain what the animals did and how they behaved.

2. Do you know of any other animals that can be taught to communicate with people in some way? Do animals communicate with each other? How? Give several examples to explain your answer.

3. Have you ever tried training an animal to do something? What were the problems involved?

4. Some experts feel that training like Koko's can give animals a way to communicate their natural personalities to us. Other experts think that animals who are trained like Koko are simply imitating their trainers. Which opinion do you think is correct? Give several reasons to explain your answer. You may use examples from this article.

5. Many animals living in zoos today, including the gorilla, are threatened or endangered species. The gorilla's natural habitat, for instance, is being changed into farms, cities, and industrial centers, leaving the gorilla with no jungle to live in. What should be done about this situation for gorillas, elephants, tigers, and other threatened species? Are zoos the best place to house these animals? Do you think animals should have the right to live in their natural habitat? Does it matter to you if an animal becomes extinct?

6. Paragraph 6 describes intelligence tests. Was this test fair to Koko? Some people feel that most intelligence tests really don't measure intelligence, but instead measure a person's knowledge of local culture or situations. If a person from another culture takes this test, he or she would probably do poorly. Is this fair? Are you in favor of such tests or do you oppose them? How should a person's intelligence be tested?

J. Reading Reconstruction: Read this paragraph as many times as you can in three minutes. Then, with your book closed, try to restate the ideas in writing as clearly and completely as you can. (See exercise J in Chapter 1 for complete instructions.)

Hellion the Helper

Hellion is a small monkey. She has been trained to be the hands and feet for a man in Boston named Robert who was in a serious accident. Robert is completely paralyzed. Although a nurse cares for him, the nurse must go to work during the day. Then Hellion becomes involved. Robert turns the pages of a book with a pointer that he holds between his teeth. If he drops the pointer, Hellion instantly picks it up and puts it back in his mouth. Hellion can bring Robert a drink from the refrigerator, feed him with a spoon, turn on his record player, and comb his hair. She is intelligent and sensitive to Robert's needs. She seems to enjoy her association with humans.

Key words (to be written on the chalkboard):

Hellion	cares for	instantly	sensitive
trained	involved	record	association
paralyzed	pointer	intelligent	

Comprehension Check

On a separate piece of paper, write the numbers 1 through 10 on both sides. Mark one side "Test 1" and the other side "Test 2." Read each statement and decide whether it is true or false. Write "T" after true statements and "F" after false statements under Test 1. After you have finished the comprehension check, turn Test 1 face down. Then read the article again and do the comprehension check again under Test 2. Base your answers on the information in this article *only,* even if you disagree with what the author said.

1. Koko is a gorilla who has learned to use sign language.

2. Koko is very shy and afraid of people.

3. Koko can understand sentences that her trainer uses, but she cannot construct sentences of her own.

4. Koko's trainer is not afraid of working with her even though Koko is very strong already and will weigh 250 pounds when she is fully grown.

5. Gorillas and chimpanzees have a similar temperament and are both easy to work with.

6. Koko uses approximately 375 hand signs regularly and appropriately.

7. Koko answers IQ tests the same way as an average human child.

8. Koko can define objects.

9. Koko seems to know how to lie.

10. Koko thinks she is a human being because she has lived with her trainer for so many years.

Review Examination I (Chapters 1, 2, 3, and 4)

A.   Content Summary: Complete the following statements. (20 points: 5 points each)

1. The main idea of *Two More Billion People by Century's End* is that:

2. A recent change in Kuwait is that many more women:

3. Name at least five things you can do to induce sleep.

4. Koko is remarkable because:

B.   Word Forms: Look at the first word in each line. Write the appropriate form of this word in the sentence that follows it. Be careful to use appropriate verb tenses, singular and plural forms for nouns, and passive voice where necessary. (40 points: 2 points each)

(Example)

manager   How did you _manage_ to finish in time?

1. increase   There will be a huge _____ in population by the end of the century.

2. hope   Are there any _____ signs in this gloomy situation?

3. grow   The graphs predict _____ patterns, and they should be studied carefully.

4. project   It _____ that nearly 80 percent of all people will live in less developed countries by the year 2000.

5. solve   Are these overpopulation problems _____ ?

6. equal   Women in Kuwait are struggling for _____ .

7. progress   It is true that they have made _____ toward their goal.

8. educate   For example, many more women are becoming _____ than before.

9. choice   Kuwaiti men may _____ to marry educated women in the future, but they have not done so up to now.

10. legal   Dr. al-Awadhi is a lawyer, and she is the first female _____ professor at the University of Kuwait.

11. cure   Here is good news for insomnia sufferers: Insomnia is _____ without drugs.

12. probable   If you can't sleep, there are _____ things bothering you.

13. **anxiety**   Do you feel _____ about something?

14. **breath**   Difficulty in _____ may be related to insomnia.

15. **belief**   If you suffer from insomnia, it is important to _____ that you can do something about it.

16. **intelligence**   You have to admit that Koko is a very _____ gorilla!

17. **sense**   Some of her responses were quite _____ .

18. **argument**   Sometimes Koko _____ with her trainer.

19. **instant**   Also Koko didn't tell the truth in all _____ .

20. **involve**   The _____ between Koko and her trainer was both obvious and touching.

C. Cloze: Choose the most appropriate word for each blank. (10 points: 1 point each)

Overpopulation is one of the most serious problems facing us. The world's exploding population (1) _____ even more growing pains (2) _____ for already crowded areas.
(signals—predicts—experiences)
(before—now—ahead)

(3) _____ new United Nations study (4) _____ that
(The—Some—A)
(signals—forecasts—tells)

by the year (5) _____ 2 billion persons will
(2000—1982—1900)

(6) _____ added to the 4.4 (7) _____ in the
(have—be—not be)
(million—billion—thousand)

world today. (8) _____ more troubling than the
(Even—Far—No)

(9) _____ number of inhabitants are (10) _____
(big—small—increasing)
(a—the—these)

projections of where they will be concentrated.

D. Composition: Write a composition about *one* of these topics. (30 points)

1. In order to curb population growth, governments should encourage people to have fewer children by giving them specific rewards for having fewer children. Do you agree or disagree? What kinds of rewards or incentives would encourage people to have fewer children? Do you know of countries where people are encouraged to have fewer children through positive benefits? Are these population control programs effective? Why? Or why not?

2. Women should not have careers because they offer a greater service to their families and to society by staying at home with their children. No one can give the same quality of care and attention to children as their mothers can. Do you agree or disagree? Why? Please give reasons and examples to illustrate your position.

3. Since gorillas will never be able to communicate as effectively as humans do, is there any really good reason for spending so much time and money to teach them a little bit of language? If so, why? If not, why not? Please give reasons and examples to illustrate your position.

5

Before you read, here are some questions to think about:

— Have you ever looked for a job? If so, what did you do?

— If you were looking for a job now, what would you do? Why?

— If you were hiring someone for a job, what qualifications would you look for? What kind of person would you want to hire?

— What advice would you give someone who is looking for a job?

HOW TO FIND A JOB

[Jerrold G. Simon, Ed.D., psychologist and career development specialist at the Harvard Business School, has counseled a great many people in their search for jobs. Here are some practical suggestions he has for getting the job you want.]

1   If you are about to launch a search for a job, the suggestions I offer here can help you, whether or not you have a high school or college diploma, whether you are just starting out or changing your job or career in midstream.

"What do I want to do?"

2   Before you try to find a job opening, you have to answer the hardest question of your working life: "What do I want to do?" Here's a good way. Sit down with a piece of paper and don't get up till you've listed all the things you're proud to have accomplished. Your list might include being head of a fund-raising campaign or acting a juicy role in the senior play.

3   Study the list. You'll see a pattern emerge of the things you do best and like to do best. You might discover that you're happiest working with people, or maybe with numbers, or words. Whatever it is, you'll see it. Once you've decided what job area to go after, read more about it in the reference section of your library. "Talk shop" with any people you know in that field. Then start to get your resume together.

Writing a resume

4   There are many good books that offer sample resumes and describe widely used formats. The one that is still most popular, the *reverse chronological*, emphasizes where you worked and the jobs and titles you held.

5   Your name and address go at the top and also your phone number. What job do you want? That's what a prospective employer looks for first. If you know exactly, list that next under *Job Objective*. Otherwise, save it for your cover letter (I describe that later) when you're writing for a specific job to a specific person. In any case, make sure your resume focuses on the kind of work you can do and want to do.

6   Now comes *Work Experience*. Here's where you list your qualifications. *Lead with your most important credentials.* If you've had a distinguished work history in an area related to the job you're seeking, lead off with that. If your education will impress the prospective employer more, start with that. Begin with your most recent experience first and work backwards. Include your titles or positions held and list the years.

Figures don't brag

7   The most qualified people don't always get the job. It goes to the person who presents himself most persuasively in person and on paper. So don't just list where you were and what you did. This is your chance to tell *how well you did*. Were you the best salesman? Did you cut operating costs? Give numbers, statistics, percentages, increases in sales or profits.

No job experience?

8   In that case, list your summer jobs, extracurricular school activities, honors, and awards. Choose the activities that will enhance your qualifications for the job.

9   Next list your *Education*—unless you chose to start with that. This should also be in reverse chronological order. List your high school only if you didn't go on to college. Include college degree, postgraduate degrees, dates conferred, major and minor courses you took that help qualify you for the job you want. Also, did you pay your own way? Earn scholarships or fellowships? Those are impressive accomplishments.

No diplomas or degrees?

10   Then tell about your education: special training programs or courses that can qualify you. Describe outside activities that reveal your talents and abilities. Did you sell the most tickets to the annual charity musical? Did you take your motorcycle engine apart and put it back together so it works? These can help you.

11   Next list any *Military Service*. This could lead off your resume if it is your only work experience. Stress skills learned, promotions earned, leadership shown.

12   Now comes *Personal Data*. This is your chance to let the reader get a glimpse of the personal you and to further the image you've worked to project in the preceding sections. For example, if you're after a job in computer programming, and you enjoy playing chess, mention it. Chess playing requires the ability to think through a problem. Include foreign languages spoken, extensive travel, particular interests or professional memberships, *if* they advance your cause.

No typos please

13   Keep your writing style simple. Be brief. Start sentences with impressive action verbs: "Created," "Designed," "Achieved," "Caused."

Make sure your grammar and spelling are correct. And no typos! Use 8½" × 11" bond paper—white or off-white for easy reading. Don't cram things together. Make sure your original is clean and readable. Then have it professionally duplicated. Don't make carbon copies.

Get it into the right hands

14   Now that your resume is ready, start to track down job openings. How? Look up business friends, personal friends, neighbors, your minister, your college alumni association, or professional services. Keep up with trade publications, and read help-wanted ads. Start your own "direct mail" campaign. First, find out about the companies you are interested in—their size, location, what they make, their competition, their advertising, their prospects. Get their annual report—and read it.

No "Dear Sir" letters

15   Send your resume, along with a cover letter, to a specific person in the company, not to "Gentlemen" or "Dear Sir." The person should be the top person in the area where you want to work. Spell his name properly! The cover letter should appeal to your reader's own needs. What's in it for him? Quickly explain why you are approaching *his* company (their product line, their superior training program) and what you can bring to the company. Back up your claims with facts. Then refer him to your enclosed resume and ask for an interview.

An interview!

16   And now you've got an interview! Be sure to call the day before to confirm it. Meantime, *prepare yourself.* Research the company and the job by reading books and business journals in the library. On the big day, arrive 15 minutes early. Act calm, even though, if you're normal, you're trembling inside at 6.5 on the Richter scale. At every chance, let your interviewer see that your personal skills and qualifications relate to the job at hand. If it's a sales position, for example, go all out to show how articulate and persuasive you are. Afterwards, follow through with a brief thank-you note. This is a fine opportunity to restate your qualifications and add any important points you didn't get a chance to bring up during the interview.

Keep good records

17   Keep a list of prospects. List the dates you contacted them, when they replied and what was said. And remember, someone out there is looking for someone *just like you*. It takes hard work and sometimes luck to find that person. Keep at it and you'll succeed.

TURN TO COMPREHENSION CHECK AT END OF CHAPTER

1500 words

READING TIMES: READING SPEED:
1st reading _____ minutes   15 minutes = 100 wpm
2nd reading _____ minutes   10 minutes = 150 wpm
                                   8 minutes = 188 wpm
                                   7 minutes = 214 wpm

A. Analysis of Ideas and Relationships: Circle the letter next to the best answer.

1. The subject of this article is:
   a. Jerrold G. Simon, Ed.D.
   b. how to try to get the job you really want.
   c. how to write a resume.

   Please explain your answer.

2. Dr. Simon wrote this article for:
   a. college graduates with or without experience.
   b. high school graduates with or without work experience.
   c. both (a) and (b)

   Give examples from the article to support your answer.

3. Put these activities in the order in which Dr. Simon suggests:
   a. go for an interview
   b. send out your resume to companies
   c. write a cover letter for your resume and ask for an interview
   d. decide what you want to do
   e. find out everything you can about the field
   f. write your resume
   g. get an interview

4. Put these items in **reverse chronological order**:
   a. Hunter High School, 1975–78
   b. Hunter College, 1980–82
   c. Queens College, Summer 1980
   d. Manhattan Community College, 1978–80
   e. The Graduate Center of the City University of New York, 1982–

   (No final date indicates **still in attendance**.)

5. If you wanted an entry-level job in architecture, which hobby would you list on your resume? Why?
   a. Swimming.
   b. Photography.
   c. Reading.

6. Why should you list military service (if you have it) on your resume?
   a. To stress skills learned and other achievements in the service.
   b. To show that you are patriotic.
   c. To explain those years of your life.

7. Your cover letter should begin:
   a. Dear Mr. Lurie:
   b. To Whom It May Concern:
   c. Dear Sir:

   Why?

8. Put the following statements into logical order. Then refer to paragraph 15 to check your work.
   a. "Spell his name properly!"
   b. "Send your resume, along with a cover letter, to a specific person in the company, not to 'Gentlemen' or 'Dear Sir.' "
   c. "The person should be the top person in the area where you want to work."
   d. "The cover letter should appeal to your reader's own needs."
   e. "What's in it for him?"

9. Check "Yes" or "No" for these statements:

	Yes	No
a. If your interview is at 9, you should arrive exactly at 9.	___	___
b. Find out everything you can about the company and the job before the interview.	___	___
c. Let the interviewer do all the talking.	___	___
d. Try to act calm.	___	___
e. Write a short thank-you note to the interviewer later.	___	___

   Please explain all of your answers.

10. Which advice is NOT appropriate to give to someone looking for a job?
    a. Just sit back and wait and something will come along.
    b. If at first you don't succeed, try, try again.
    c. Don't give up.

B. **Interpretation of Words and Phrases:** Circle the letter next to the best answer.

   1. **Keep up** your hard work while you are looking for a job.
      a. Continue
      b. Stop
      c. Don't do

2. In the interview, **bring up** everything in your education and experience that may be related to the job.
   a. mention
   b. remember
   c. write down

3. Go to the library and **look up information about** your field of interest.
   a. study
   b. research
   c. think about

4. **Find out** the name of the division or department head and send your cover letter and resume directly to that person.
   a. Figure out
   b. Remember
   c. Discover

5. **Go all out** in your job search.
   a. Go to a lot of places
   b. Do everything you can
   c. Talk to a lot of people

6. At the interview, be sure to explain what you can **bring to** the job.
   a. contribute to
   b. earn on
   c. learn on

7. In your resume, **lead off with** your most important accomplishments.
   a. end with
   b. underline
   c. start with

8. **Track down** information on job openings.
   a. Search for
   b. Follow
   c. Think about

9. **Follow through with** suggestions people give you for finding a job.
   a. Listen to and take
   b. Go after
   c. Search for

10. **Keep at** your job search.
    a. Do
    b. Don't stop
    c. Hold onto

C. Synonyms: From this list choose a synonym for the word in bold type in each sentence. Use appropriate tenses for verbs and singular or plural forms for nouns.

to talk about work	related	possible, future
to begin	in charge of	to crowd
to shake	to advance	typing mistake
		short

1. Here are some things to think about before you **launch** your job search.

2. Be sure to tell a **prospective** employer what kind of job you want.

3. Find people who are working in your field of interest and **talk shop** with them.

4. Make sure that your resume looks clean and neat and that it doesn't have any **typos** in it.

5. Don't try to **cram** too much information on a page.

6. If you were **head** of a project or committee, be sure to mention it.

7. Include any work, educational, and personal experience you have that will **further** the image you are trying to project.

8. Be sure to mention all **relevant** experience.

9. When you go for an interview, try to appear calm even if you are **trembling**.

10. Afterwards, write a **brief** thank-you note.

D. Prepositions and Verb-Completers: Write any appropriate preposition or verb-completer in the blank spaces.

1. Before you start _____ look _____ a job, you should think _____ what you want _____ do.

2. Go _____ the library and look _____ information _____ any fields you are interested _____ .

3. Talk _____ as many people as possible _____ their jobs and the kind _____ work they do.

4. Be sure your resume focuses _____ the kind _____ work you can do and want _____ do.

5. Start _____ _____ your most important credentials.

6. Put the information _____ reverse chronological order.

7. Put _____ any relevant experience or interests.

8. Find _____ the name _____ the person you should send your resume and cover letter _____ .

9. Try _____ act calm _____ the interview.

10. Think _____ some questions _____ ask your interviewers.

E. **Cloze Exercise: Select the best word to fill in each blank. Sometimes there may be more than one possible answer.**

   If you are about to launch a search for a job, the suggestions I offer here can help you, whether or not you have a high school diploma, whether you are just starting out or changing your job or career in midstream. Before you try to (1)_____ a job opening, you (2)_____ to
   (find—search—apply)   (must—should—have)
   answer the hardest (3)_____ of your working life:
   (thing—question—statement)
   (4)_____ do I want to (5)_____?" Here's a good
   (When—What—Why)   (do—work—have)
   way. (6)_____ down with a piece (7)_____ paper and
   (Start—Write—Sit)   (clean—of—white)
   don't get (8)_____ till you've listed all (9)_____
   (finished—done—up)   (the—many—some)
   things you're proud to (10)_____ accomplished. Your list might
   (be—have—had)
   (11)_____ being head of a (12)_____ -raising
   (be—have—include)   (charity—fund—money)
   campaign, or acting (13)_____ juicy role in the senior play.
   (a—the—this)

F. **Resume Writing: Rearrange Jackson O'Keefe's resume by changing the order of the categories and by using reverse chronological order (the most recent dates first) within the categories. Number the blanks on the left side of the resume to indicate the order you desire. You may use Renata Martell's resume for a guide if you wish (p. 80). You do not have to follow this order, however. Please be prepared to explain why you ordered Jackson's resume as you did.**

_1_   JACKSON O'KEEFE
Chapel Road
Bennington, Vermont 05201
802-442-9612

_____ **Personal Interests:**
Skiing, tennis, soccer, and swimming.

_____ **Education:**

_____ 1981 Graduated from Mt. Anthony High School, Bennington, Vermont 05201 with B+ average.

_____ 1981– Attending the University of Vermont, Burlington, Vermont. Majoring in Physical Education and Psychology.

_____ **Job Objective:**   To work as sports director of a camp.

_____ **References:**

Jack Padilla	Maria and Kurt Vail
Director	Directors
Camp Arrowhead	Camp Bald Mountain
Box 639	Bald Mountain, Vermont
Lake Arrowhead,	05304
California 45879	

_____ **Honors and Awards:**

_____ 1979 Placed second in the 100-yard competition. Vermont State High School Meet.

_(2)_ 1980 Placed first in the 50-yard competition. Vermont State High School Meet.

_____ 1980 Placed second in the 100-yard competition. New England Swim Meet.

_(1)_ 1982 Placed first in 50-yard competition. University of Vermont Spring Meet.

_____ **Experience:**

_____ 1982 Camp Bald Mountain, Bald Mountain, Vermont
Directed and supervised swimming program for 300 camper camp for boys from 12 to 16. Supervised staff of six swimming instructors. Organized water carnival for parents' day: a 15-event competition open to campers of all ages.

_____ 1981 Camp Arrowhead, Lake Arrowhead, California
Worked as senior counselor in co-ed camp for 200 boys and girls from 10 to 18. Supervised 14-year-old boys. Taught senior life saving and advanced swimming and played on camp water polo team.

RENATA MARTELL
26 East 9th Street, Apt. 5B
New York, New York 10011
212-632-6098

Career Objective: To design costumes for the theatre, movies, or opera.

Experience:

1982 to   Career-World, Inc. 641 Seventh Avenue, New York, New York
present   *Designer-Stylist:* Create and design dresses and suits for the professional woman in medium-price range. Work with production department in meeting production schedules. Help produce quarterly shows for buyers.

1980 to   Couture du Monde. 411 Madison Avenue, New York, New York
1982   *Design Assistant:* Assisted head designers in copying dress styles from Paris, Rome, Madrid, and London. Assisted in adapting styles to meet the needs of the American market.

1979 to   Couture du Monde. 411 Madison Avenue, New York, New York
1980   *Model:* Modeled couture designs from Paris, Rome, Madrid, and London.

Education:

1979   Fashion Institute of Technology, New York, New York
A.A. Degree in fashion designing.

Honors:

1979   Received first prize in theatrical costume design: ball gown for Mimi in *La Boheme.*

Personal Interests:

Theatre, opera, chamber music, and art.
Performed in operettas and plays in high school.

References:

References and portfolio are available upon request.

G. **Word Forms:** Choose the correct word form to fit into each sentence referring to the chart as necessary. Use appropriate verb tenses, singular or plural forms for nouns, and passive voice where necessary.

Noun	*Verb*	*Adjective*	*Adverb*
accomplishment	to accomplish	accomplished	
actor	to act	active	actively
act			
action			
activity			
competitor	to compete	competing	
competition		competitive	competitively
decision	to decide	decisive	decisively
		deciding	decidedly
discoverer	to discover	discovered	
discovery			
experience	to experience	experienced	
persuasion	to persuade	persuasive	persuasively
qualification	to qualify	qualifying	
		qualified	
referral	to refer		
reference			
suggestion	to suggest		

1. **suggestion, to suggest**
   a. What do you _____ ?
   b. I took his _____ .

2. **experience, to experience, experienced**
   a. It's easier to get a job if you have _____ .
   b. She was an _____ writer.
   c. Did you _____ any discomfort?

3. **accomplishment, to accomplish, accomplished**
   a. List your most important _____ on your resume.
   b. How did you _____ so much in so little time?
   c. He is an _____ pianist, and he gives concerts all over the world.

4. **referral, reference, to refer**
   a. I don't understand what you are _____ to.
   b. You will have to get a _____ from your doctor.
   c. You can find the dictionaries and encyclopedias in the general _____ room at the library.

5. **qualification, to qualify, qualifying, qualified**
   a. Are you sure he is a _____ surgeon?
   b. I am going to check his _____ for the position.
   c. I am very busy studying for my Ph.D. _____ exams, so I can't go to a disco tonight.
   d. Would you care to _____ your remarks in any way?

6. **decision, to decide, decisive, deciding, decisively, decidedly**
   a. She certainly knows how to act in a _____ manner.
   b. Hurry up and make a _____ on that matter.
   c. She _____ to tell him the truth.
   d. "No," she replied _____ .
   e. He was _____ thinner than he had been the year before.
   f. What were the _____ factors?

7. **persuasion, to persuade, persuasive, persuasively**
   a. He is a very _____ speaker.
   b. He spoke very _____ .
   c. She has great powers of _____ .
   d. I was _____ to change my mind, much to my surprise.

8. **discoverer, discovery, to discover, discovered**
   a. Who were the first _____ of the North American continent?
   b. The recently _____ oil has greatly aided their economy.
   c. It was an important _____ .
   d. I _____ my wallet was missing when I opened my bag.

9. **competitor, competition, to compete, competing, competitive, competitively**
   a. Did you watch the World Cup Soccer _____ ?
   b. West Germany and Italy _____ for first place in 1982.
   c. How many _____ were there in all?
   d. The _____ teams looked each other over carefully.
   e. She definitely has a _____ spirit.
   f. Do you play tennis _____ ?

10. **actor, act, action, activity, to act, active, actively**
    a. What was the basis for his strong _____ ?
    b. Don't _____ surprised. You knew all along.
    c. We didn't like the play, so we left after the first _____ .
    d. What an _____ child!

e. She was _____ opposed to the war, and she took part in the peace movement.

f. He is an unemployed _____ .

g. Her life is full of _____ , so it's impossible to get a minute alone with her.

H. **Sentence Paraphrase: Make new sentences using these sentence frames, and then make up your own sentences. You may add or leave out words, but try to retain the meaning of the original sentences.**

1. According to Dr. Simon, the hardest question to answer is, "What do I want to do?"

   Dr. Simon _____ is, " _____

   _____ ?"

   Other possible sentences:

2. Dr. Simon recommends that you make a list of your accomplishments, study this list until you see a pattern of interest emerging, and then go to the library to research your field of interest.

   Dr. Simon _____ do these things:

   (1) _____ ,

   (2) _____ ,

   and (3) _____ .

   Other possible sentences:

3. It's a good idea to arrive 15 minutes early for an interview.

   Try _____ .

   Other possible sentences:

I.   Topics for Discussion and Composition

1. How does this article relate to your personal experience? Have you ever conducted a job search? If so, how did you organize your search? Did you get any new ideas from this article? How would you organize a job search now?

2. This article discusses how to get a job in the United States. In other countries, however, there are different ways of getting jobs. How do people get jobs in your country? Explain and give specific examples if you can.

3. Make a list of the most important accomplishments of your life. Show your list to someone else in your class and discuss with this person the kinds of job possibilities that are suggested by your list.

4. Following the advice given in the article, write your own resume. Try to keep it to one page if possible.

J.   Reading Reconstruction: Read this paragraph as many times as you can in three minutes. Then, with your book closed, try to restate the ideas in writing as clearly and completely as you can. (See exercise J in Chapter 1 for complete instructions.)

Getting Ready for the Interview

Interviews are important, and you should prepare for them carefully. Before you go, try to find out as much as you can about the company and also the job opening. Think carefully about your qualifications in terms of this job. What could you bring to the job? Be sure to think of some questions you have about the job and the company. This shows your interest and makes a good impression on the interviewer. Finally, be sure to dress appropriately and arrive 15 minutes early for the interview. Good luck!

Key words (to be written on the chalkboard):

interviews	company	questions	interviewer
important	job opening	interest	dress appropriately
prepare	qualifications	impression	arrive
find out			

Comprehension Check

On a separate piece of paper, write the numbers 1 through 10 on both sides. Mark one side "Test 1" and the other side "Test 2." Read each statement and decide whether it is true or false. Write "T" after true statements and "F" after false statements under Test 1. After you have finished the comprehension check, turn Test 1 face down. Then read the article again and do the comprehension check again under Test 2. Base your answers on the information in this article *only,* even if you disagree with what the author said.

1. This article is written only for college graduates.

2. The first thing you have to do in your job search is to figure out what you want to do.

3. The most popular form for a resume is *chronological:* you begin with your first job experience (or school) and continue on from there.

4. You should put your name, address, and phone number at the bottom of the page on your resume.

5. Under the education section, you should mention special training programs and non-credit courses as well as credit courses.

6. The author of this article recommends that you do not mention military service on your resume.

7. It is a good idea to mention hobbies and special interests—if they are related in any way to your field of interest.

8. You should begin your cover letter: "Dear Sir."

9. You should call the day before your interview to confirm it.

10. You should arrive 15 minutes early for your interview.

6

Before you read, here are some questions to think about:

- What place does work have in a person's life?
- Which is more important to you: salary and benefits or job security?
- Would you like the idea of working for the same company all your working life? Why? Or why not?
- Would you always be loyal to your company—if you knew they would always be loyal to you?

MADE IN JAPAN:
A DAY IN THE LIFE OF A
TYPICAL JAPANESE WORKER

1 It is 6:15 A.M. and a cool, cloudy dawn envelops the aging Kawasaki company housing complex in the port city of Kobe, Japan, where Yoshiaki Morita lives with his wife and two small children. Morita, 32, is awake and reading the paper as he waits for breakfast: an omelet, *miso* soup, rice, salad, and green tea. It is cold in the unheated two-room apartment, and he sits with his legs tucked under the *kotatsu*— a low table with an electric heating unit on the underside, a blanket across the top, and a table top over that. In winter, Japanese families gather for hours around this little island of warmth, eating, drinking tea, watching television, or playing games.

2 After breakfast, Morita dresses in the room where his children are still sleeping. He emerges in a brown pin-stripe suit, sweater vest, red tie, and tan, Italianate shoes. He seems a bit overdressed for a man who installs pipes in rail cars for a living. But, he says philosophically, it is good to dress well. If you dress as an inferior person, he says, you will behave as an inferior person.

3 Morita is off to Kawasaki Heavy Industries, where he will spend the day beneath the frame of a red, white, and blue trolley. Promptly at 6:55 A.M., Morita leaves his third-floor walk-up apartment, striding briskly down a walkway past the worn stone statue of Jizo, protector of children, beside a chattering, rock-filled brook. Both the statue and the brook have been there for centuries, and the builders of the housing complex took care to preserve them.

4 At the commuter train station, a ten-minute walk away, he flashes his transit pass—a fringe benefit from Kawasaki that lets him ride free. The station looks much like a commuter train station in the United States, except that it is clean, odorless, and graffiti-free. And there is one added touch: fish swim in a little pool in the miniature stylized garden bordering the station.

5 This morning, as every morning, the train arrives promptly at 7:11 A.M. and drops him seventeen minutes later at Hyogo station, a few blocks from work. Morita's pace quickens as he nears his destination. He breaks into a run to avoid being late. Inside, he shifts his time card to the

"present" side but doesn't put it in the time clock. It is assumed, correctly for the most part, that no employee is late. The workers punch their time cards only on leaving, for overtime calculations.

6   When the 8:00 A.M. starting whistle blows, Morita and a couple of hundred other workers—who have changed in a locker room into clean gray cotton coveralls that Kawasaki issues once a year—form uneven rows in a yard between two shops, avoiding three sets of railroad tracks. For five minutes they do exercises—arm swings, toe touches, knee bends, and the like—to recorded instructions from a soft, female voice. No one is forced to do these exercises. Everyone does them.

7   Afterward, the workers—a handful are women—report to their units for talks from the foremen, in Morita's case, the chief of No. 1 Pipefitting, a 53-year-old man with dark hair and a smile that reveals a gold tooth. "It's a fine day," he begins conversationally, standing with his hands behind his back, "but it's getting chilly. When weather changes so quickly, take care not to catch cold." His voice turns serious. "Yesterday, quality control inspectors caught some minor defects. Make sure you recheck your work. Be 100 percent sure, so we can send it to the next shop 100 percent perfect."

8   Later, in No. 1 Pipefitting, Morita crouches under a "Septacar" hoisted three feet from the ground, its underside illuminated by a droplight. The kerosene stoves placed here and there barely dent the numbing cold in the drafty plant. On an engineering drawing, Morita has outlined his route in red like a road map. Each piece of pipe is numbered to correspond to its place. With time out for lunch and meetings, he will spend the day fitting and gluing gaskets to precut, prethreaded iron pipes, and screwing and clamping them in place.

9   At 9:40 A.M., Morita consults his watch and then hurries to a meeting with a dozen other men. They learn that results have been announced in the most recent quality control (QC) competition. In the previous year this group submitted 453 suggestions for ways to improve their job procedures; 199 were accepted. Morita notes this fact in a small black notebook in which he records his QC suggestions, details of how he accomplished difficult work assignments, and his amount of overtime. (Last fall Morita's group won 150,000 yen—about $750—in a plant-wide quality control contest. They bought themselves new uniforms with some of the money and used the rest for a three-day camping trip.)

10   On yet another day a quality control circle is meeting in a corner of the metal fabrication unit. Seated on folding chairs around a blackboard, this group is discussing the extrusion of aluminum material. Their words are barely audible above the background roar of the plant, but more significant is their animation and involvement. Individuals

leap to their feet to make points and engage each other in discussion with the enthusiasm of a group rehashing last night's ballgame.

11   Multiply this system hundreds of times and you have literally thousands of QC circles meeting throughout Japan, continually churning out suggestions for the betterment of plants and offices. Quality control is a key feature in Japanese industry. Over the years, Morita has submitted 200 suggestions; 130 have been accepted. They are small things perhaps, like changing the location of a joint so it could be more easily reached, but ones that made sense and could be formulated only by someone as familiar with the work as the man who does it. Often it took no more than a phone call to the engineering department to get an okay on the change and put it into effect almost immediately. Through the chain of command, quality control is encouraged for its ultimate values: it keeps workers interested in their work, and it saves money. Each year there is a national competition for Japan's top quality control award.

12   Morita has been back at work for two hours when the noon whistle announces lunch. Workers stream into the lunchrooms and grab two shallow red and black boxes apiece, one brimming with rice, the other containing vegetables and fish. Pots of hot tea are already on the long tables. Lunch costs 319 yen ($1.56), of which Kawasaki pays 40 percent and bills the worker for the rest on his paycheck.

13   Not much of the noon hour is spent eating. At 12:10 P.M., workers begin hurrying out nearly as fast as they hurried in. Outside, a minor Olympics seems to be taking place. Foursomes engage in fast-paced games of tenni-pong, a game played with paddles and a low net. In the open area where exercises took place that morning, workers have organized games of softball. Inside the No. 1 Pipefitting unit, badminton nets and Ping-Pong tables have been set up between the giant train bodies. During the summer, Morita can be found out on Kawasaki's tennis court; he is top-ranked on the company team. Today he chooses to join ten or so men grouped around one of the kerosene heaters. Some talk, others nap and two are playing *shogi,* a kind of chess. Work resumes at 1:00 P.M. with another set of exercises.

14   Morita's day ends at 5:00 P.M. Often there is an hour or two of overtime, but tonight he heads straight for the plant's steaming baths. Homeward bound, Morita retraces his morning route, hurrying through the darkening streets to his apartment.

15   For his labors, Morita is paid $773 each month, and twice a year he receives bonuses—equal, in the current good times, to two months' pay—giving him a yearly base salary of $12,638. He can count on overtime—nearly $300 in a typical recent month—to add to that. His taxes are much lower than those in most industrialized countries; in that

same recent month, he paid just $13.61 federal tax and $7.36 Kobe tax. His largest deduction was $56.88 toward his pension, followed by $32.20 for health insurance and $31.72 for rent in Kawasaki's housing. That's cheap rent, of course, but it buys an apartment that amounts to something less than those supplied by American public housing: in addition to a tiny kitchen, the Moritas have just two small rooms plus a small bathroom. The Moritas can stay in the company housing for only ten years; they've been there for four, so they're saving for the Japanese version of a modest condominium.

16   Morita's career is unlikely to take him past the post of foreman. He is not a college graduate and passed up the chance to go to evening college. But, he says, career advancement isn't everything. "If you work hard, it will come back in some way. You will have ability and self-confidence. Life is not only 'getting ahead'." If Morita felt any differently, he probably would be unhappy within the Japanese system, which is so structured that "getting ahead" of contemporaries is difficult. The image of a career ladder precisely fits Japanese employment; with rare exceptions, one can neither skip a rung nor leap from one ladder to another, but by the same token, once on the ladder, a worker is guaranteed a place for life: seldom is anyone fired or laid off.

17   In many respects, Morita's life is inseparable from the company. Not only does he live and work amid a Kawasaki clan, he can vacation for three dollars a day at one of a dozen Kawasaki resorts, shop at a Kawasaki company store, and buy a home through the Kawasaki real estate company. Small wonder that Morita assesses the chance of his leaving the company as "never."

18   Morita also belongs to what Americans would regard as a company union; like most Japanese workers, however, Morita has never participated in a work stoppage or strike. In general, labor peace has prevailed for two decades under a pact between industry and labor to work together for prosperity. This attitude is perhaps best summed up in a remark by the president of the Kawasaki Heavy Industries Union, Koichi Tomoigawa: "We want the company to have a profit because half goes to the company and half goes to the worker."

19   So ends another day for Yoshiaki Morita. On arriving home, where dinner is waiting, he changes from his suit into casual clothes and sits at the *kotatsu* to read the evening paper. His two-year-old daughter, Satoko, climbs eagerly into his lap. When his five-year-old son, Yoshimasa, comes into the room, Morita gives the boy a small gift-wrapped package. Yoshimasa excitedly rips it open. It is a small notebook of blank pages. It comes from the Kawasaki union for entering a drawing contest, even though Yoshimasa won no prizes.

20   Japan is like that. You do not have to be the best or the brightest to share in the goodies. You must simply do your best. By day's end Morita's Zen-like observation, "If you work hard, it will come back in some way," has become more understandable.

TURN TO COMPREHENSION CHECK AT END OF CHAPTER

1800 words

READING TIMES:
1st reading _____ minutes
2nd reading_____ minutes

READING SPEED:
15 minutes = 120 wpm
13 minutes = 138 wpm
10 minutes = 180 wpm
 8 minutes = 225 wpm

A. **Analysis of Ideas and Relationships: Circle the letter next to the best answer or supply information as asked.**

1. This article focuses on the relationship of a typical Japanese worker to:
   a. his company.
   b. his family.
   c. his society.

   Why do you think so?

2. Mr. Morita's manner of dressing (see paragraph 2) shows that:
   a. he takes pride in himself.
   b. he wishes that he had a better job.
   c. he wants people to think that he has a higher position than he does.
   Please explain your answer.

3. Please reread paragraph 3. This paragraph shows a pleasing combination of old and new. Name two old things and one new thing mentioned in this paragraph:

   _____

   _____

   What do you think this combination says about Japanese culture?

4. Paragraph 4 discusses Japanese subway stations. What does it imply, **but not directly state,** about American subway stations?

_____

   What kind of atmosphere is created in the Japanese station? Where would you rather begin your day? Why?

5. Put the following statements into logical order. Then refer to paragraph 6 to check your work.
   a. "No one is forced to do these exercises."
   b. "For five minutes they do exercises—arm swings, toe touches, knee bends, and the like—to recorded instructions from a soft, female voice."
   c. "When the 8:00 A.M. starting whistle blows, Morita and a couple of hundred other workers—who have changed in a locker room into clean gray cotton coveralls that Kawasaki issues once a year—form uneven rows in a yard between two shops, avoiding three sets of railroad tracks."

6. Paragraph 8 gives the reader an idea of:
   a. Mr. Morita's job.
   b. the careful way Mr. Morita does his job.
   c. both (a) and (b)

7. Paragraph 10 is an example of:
   a. a quality control meeting of workers.
   b. a general group discussion.
   c. a management-level quality control meeting.

8. Which statement is NOT necessarily true?
   a. Japanese workers are involved in the decision-making process through their quality control meetings.
   b. In general, Japanese workers have a closer relationship with their companies than workers in most other industrialized countries do.
   c. Japanese workers have the highest standard of living of workers anywhere in the world.

9. The writer of this article describes one day in Mr. Morita's life to show:
   a. how unique and unusual Mr. Morita is.
   b. the life of the average Japanese worker.
   c. how much more skilled and intelligent Japanese workers are.

   Please explain your answer.

10. This article was written for:
    a. a Japanese audience at the management level.
    b. a Japanese audience at the worker level.
    c. a general, non-Japanese audience.

    Please explain your answer.

B. Interpretation of Words and Phrases: Circle the letter next to the best answer.

1. The workers **churn out** suggestions in their quality control meetings.
   a. give a few
   b. give a great many
   c. reluctantly give

2. It does not take long **to get an okay** for a good proposal.
   a. to get approval
   b. to get people to agree (to)
   c. to get a suggestion

3. From their enthusiasm in the quality control meetings, you would think the workers were **rehashing** last night's ballgame.
   a. playing
   b. going to
   c. going over

4. At noon, workers **stream** into the lunchroom.
   a. hurry in great numbers
   b. slowly walk
   c. gradually go

5. After lunch, they **head straight for** the recreation area.
   a. go directly to
   b. go by
   c. go around

6. Mr. Morita can **count on** a lot of overtime each month.
   a. get paid for
   b. ask for
   c. depend on

7. He **passed up the chance** to go to college.
   a. took the chance
   b. had the chance but didn't take it
   c. didn't have the chance

8. "If you work hard, it will come back in some way."
   a. If you work hard, something will go wrong.
   b. If you work hard, you will be rewarded in some way.
   c. If you work hard, you will be promoted.

9. "Life is not only getting ahead."
   a. The main thing in life is to get promoted.
   b. It is not good to try to get a promotion.
   c. There are other important things in life besides promotions.

10. "You do not have to be the best or the brightest to share in the goodies."
   a. Even if you are not the most skilled or the smartest, you can still take part in the good life.
   b. The most skilled and the smartest get all the rewards.
   c. Even if you are not the most skilled or the brightest, you can still do your part, but you shouldn't expect any reward for it.

C. **Synonyms: From this list, choose a synonym for the word in bold type in each sentence. Use appropriate tenses for verbs and singular or plural forms for nouns.**

to keep	to come out	to start running
to walk quickly	groups of four	to last
to surround by	to begin again	exactly
excited		

1. The city **was enveloped in** an early-morning fog.

2. After breakfast, Mr. Morita **emerges** fully dressed for the day.

3. He leaves his apartment **promptly** at 6:55 A.M.

4. He **strides briskly** to the train station.

5. He **breaks into a run** as he approaches work.

6. The builders of the housing complex tried **to preserve** the statue and the brook when they built the complex.

7. In the quality control discussions, the workers become quite **animated.**

8. **Foursomes** play tenni-pong after lunch.

9. After lunch and recreation, work **resumes** at 1 P.M.

10. Labor peace **has prevailed** for two decades in Japan.

D. **Prepositions and Verb-Completers: Write any appropriate preposition or verb-completer in the blank spaces.**

1. Mr. Morita lives _____ his wife and children _____ the port city _____ Kobe, Japan.

2. He leaves his apartment promptly _____ 6:55 A.M. and walks _____ the nearby train station.

3. Near work, he breaks _____ a run _____ order _____ avoid being late.

4. _____ five minutes, everyone does exercises.

5. Afterwards, they report _____ their units _____ talks the foremen.

6. _____ 9:40 A.M., Morita hurries _____ a meeting _____ dozen other men.

7. The results _____ a recent quality control competition have been announced.

8. _____ lunch, the workers play games _____ the recreation areas.

9. Morita's workday ends _____ 5:00 P.M., although often there is an hour or two _____ overtime.

10. _____ many respects, Morita's life is inseparable _____ his company.

E. Cloze Exercise: Select the best word to fill in each blank. Sometimes there may be more than one possible answer.

It is 6:15 A.M. and a cool, cloudy dawn envelops the aging Kawasaki company housing complex in the port city of Kobe, Japan, where Yoshiaki Morita lives with his wife and two small children. Morita, 32, is awake and (1)_____ the paper as he waits for
(reading—watching—seeing)

(2)_____ : an omelet, *miso* soup, rice, salad, and green tea.
(breakfast—lunch—dinner)

(3)_____ is cold in the unheated two- (4)_____
(He—It—Weather)   (bathroom—room—story)

apartment, and he sits with (5)_____ legs tucked under the
(the—his—long)

kotatsu— (6)_____ low table with an electric
(the—a—that)

(7)_____ unit on the underside, a blanket
(blanket—heating—cooking)

(8)_____ the top, and a table top (9)_____
(under—across—beside)   (over—under—beside)

that. In winter, Japanese families (10)_____ for hours
(spend—wait—gather)

around this little (11)_____ of warmth, eating, drinking tea,
(table—island—thing)

watching television, or playing games.

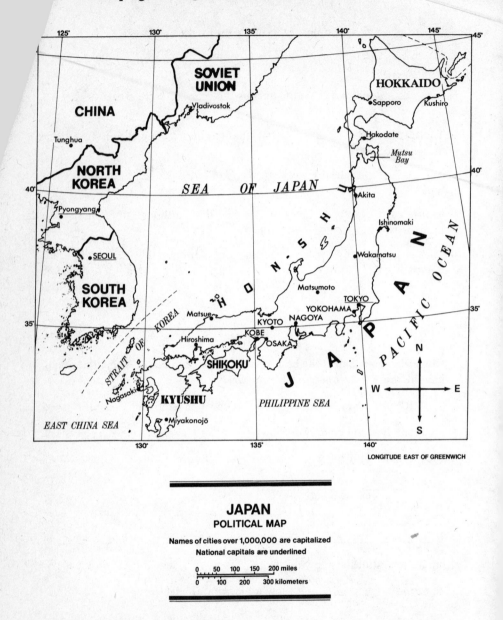

JAPAN
POLITICAL MAP

Names of cities over 1,000,000 are capitalized
National capitals are underlined

```
0    50   100  150   200 miles
0       100   200    300 kilometers
```

F. Map Reading: Look at this map of Japan and answer these questions.

1. Japan is composed of four major islands. The biggest island is *Honshu*. What are the names of the other three? _____

_____

Which island is northernmost? _____ Southernmost? _____

2. Japan is surrounded by an ocean and three seas. What is the ocean? _____
   What are the seas? _____
   Which sea is to the west of Japan? _____ To the southeast? _____

3. What is the country nearest to Japan? _____
   How far is it from Japan? _____

4. What other countries are close to Japan? _____
   Approximately how far are these countries from Japan? _____
   What direction are they from Tokyo? _____

5. How far is the island of Hokkaido from the Soviet Union? _____
   Which direction is Hokkaido from the Soviet Union? _____
   Which direction is Hokkaido from Korea? _____
   On Hokkaido, name one city that is due west of Kushiro: _____
   and one that is due north of Hakodate: _____

6. How many cities in Japan have a population of 1,000,000 or more? _____
   What are their names? _____
   How do you know which ones they are? _____

7. Approximately how far is Nagoya from Tokyo? _____
   Nagoya is to the _____ of Tokyo and to the _____ of Osaka.

8. The latitude of Kyoto is 35. What is the longitude? _____

9. What are the latitude and longitude of the northern tip of the island of Hokkaido? _____

10. Approximately how far is it from the southern tip of Kyushu to the northern tip of Hokkaido? _____ . Mutsu Bay is at the _____ tip of Honshu. The city of Nagasaki is at the _____ tip of Kyushu.

G. **Word Forms:** Choose the correct word form to fit into each sentence referring to the chart as necessary. Use appropriate verb tenses, singular or plural forms for nouns, and passive voice where necessary.

Noun	Verb	Adjective	Adverb
chill	to chill	chilly	
excitement	to excite	excited exciting excitable	excitedly
inferiority		inferior	
participant participation	to participate		
philosopher philosophy	to philosophize	philosophical	philosophically
precision preciseness		precise	precisely
profit	to profit	profitable	profitably
prosperity	to prosper	prosperous	prosperously
protector protection	to protect	protective	protectively
quality		qualitative	qualitatively

1. **philosopher, philosophy, to philosophize, philosophical, philosophically**
   a. Miguel studied _____ in Barcelona.
   b. How many Greek _____ can you name?
   c. "Oh, well," she said _____ . "We learned something important from the experience, I guess."
   d. She was by nature _____ .
   e. She loved to _____ about life and death.

2. **inferiority, inferior**
   a. Unfortunately, he suffers from an _____ complex.
   b. He has always felt _____ to other people.

3. **chill, to chill, chilly**
   a. Be careful. There's a _____ in the air.
   b. I feel a bit _____ , so I think I'll put on a sweater.
   c. Don't forget to _____ the champagne!

4. **quality, qualitative, qualitatively**
   a. Did you do a _____ analysis of this substance? We need to know its chemical composition.
   b. What is your most interesting _____ ?
   c. We can approach the matter _____ or quantitatively.

5. **prosperity, to prosper, prosperous, prosperously**
   a. Saudi Arabia is a very _____ country because of its oil.
   b. Oil has brought great _____ to the Middle East.
   c. People live much more _____ than they used to.
   d. That region began to _____ about 25 years ago.

6. **profit, to profit, profitable, profitably**
   a. The microcomputer business is very _____ now.
   b. I am sure I could _____ from your ideas.
   c. The first year the business did not make a _____ .
   d. The new president reorganized the business _____ .

7. **participant, participation, to participate**
   a. How many _____ were there in the conference?
   b. Did you _____ in any sports in school?
   c. Thank you for your _____ .

8. **excitement, to excite, exciting, excited, excitable, excitedly**
   a. What an _____ idea!
   b. It isn't good for children to have too much _____ .
   c. President Lincoln's wife was a very nervous, _____ person.
   d. Her behavior has _____ unfavorable comment.
   e. I was _____ by the unexpected news.
   f. She always talked very _____ .

9. **precision, preciseness, precise, precisely**
   a. I was impressed by the _____ of his speech.
   b. _____ is extremely important in handling this machinery.
   c. He spoke very _____ .
   d. Could you be more _____ ? I don't understand your meaning.

10. **protector, protection, to protect, protective, protectively**
    a. She put her arm around him _____ .
    b. I don't need any _____ .
    c. Jizo is known as the _____ of children in Japan.
    d. Can you _____ yourself in case of danger?
    e. Perhaps you are being too _____ .

H. Sentence Paraphrase: Make new sentences using these sentence frames, and then make up your own sentences. You may add or leave out words, but try to retain the meaning of the original sentence.

1. The working day begins with exercises. No one is forced to do these exercises. Everyone does them.

The working day _____ , and

although _____ ,

everyone _____ .

Other possible sentences:

2. The foreman said that the day before the quality control inspectors caught some minor defects, and he advised the workers to recheck their work.

The foreman said, "_____

_____ .

Please _____ ."

Other possible sentences:

3. In a number of ways, Morita's life cannot be separated from the company.

_____ respects, Morita's life _____

inseparable _____ .

Other possible sentences:

I. Topics for Discussion and Composition

1. Mr. Morita says, "Life is not only getting ahead." What do you think he means by this statement? What else is important to him? How do you know? Do you agree with him? Why? Or why not?

2. In Japan, people's lives are closely involved with their companies. People tend to stay with the same company throughout their working lives. Transportation, housing, and vacations are often partially paid for by the company. The company serves as a giant support net for the workers. What are the advantages of such a system? What are the disadvantages? Be as specific as possible.

3. Compared to the Japanese, people in Western countries tend to change jobs frequently. What are some reasons for people changing jobs? What are the advantages of changing jobs? The disadvantages? Which system would you prefer? Why?

4. If you could work for one company your entire working life, would you choose to do so? What benefits would you be willing to give up for a lifetime of job security? Would you be satisfied with a lower position if it meant you would always have a secure job? Why? Or why not? Give specific reasons and examples to support your position.

5. If you could design a company with ideal working conditions, what would these conditions be? Why? Give specific examples.

6. Discuss the quality control group system mentioned in this article. What are the company benefits of this system? Why? What are the worker benefits? Why? Be as specific as possible.

7. Have you ever had a job that deeply satisfied you? If so, describe this job and tell why it satisfied you. Compare it, if possible, to a job you did not like and discuss why you did not like the other job.

8. How important is work in the total context of life? Could you be happy without having a job? Why? Or why not? What does having a job—or not having a job—mean to you? Do you think it is necessary for healthy adults to work? Why? Or why not? Give specific reasons and examples to explain your position.

J.   Reading Reconstruction: Read this paragraph as many times as you can in three minutes. Then, with your book closed, try to restate the ideas in writing as clearly and completely as you can. (See exercise J in Chapter 1 for complete instructions.)

The Price of Sharing

The uncertain economic conditions of recent years have caused union and management representatives to explore many ways of handling labor problems. Workers have always wanted to share in the profits when the company has good times. Now management representatives are saying, "Fine. We'll share the profits with you—if you'll share the losses with us." Workers are having to decide whether they are willing to take the chance of salary and benefit cuts in bad times. They are having to decide whether job security is more important than other benefits. In effect, they are having to decide whether they are willing and able to pay the cost of sharing.

Key words (to be written on the chalkboard):

uncertain	management	workers	decide	cuts
economic	representatives	share	chance	security
conditions	labor	profits	salary	cost
union	problems	losses	benefit	sharing

Comprehension Check

On a separate piece of paper, write the numbers 1 through 10 on both sides. Mark one side "Test 1" and the other side "Test 2." Read each statement and decide whether it is true or false. Write "T" after true statements and "F" after false statements under Test 1. After you have finished the comprehension check, turn Test 1 face down. Then read the article again and do the comprehension check again under Test 2. Base your answers on the information in this article *only,* even if you disagree with what the author said.

1. Japanese workers have bigger apartments than American workers do.

2. Mr. Morita's primary motivation for working hard at his job is to get ahead: to be promoted over his fellow workers.

3. Quality control meetings allow workers to participate in the decision-making process.

4. Workers voluntarily participate in the warm-up exercises before work.

5. Mr. Morita wears his work clothes to and from work.

6. Japanese workers have less job security than American workers do.

7. Japanese workers are seldom laid off or fired.

8. Labor strikes are common in Japan.

9. The Japanese system rewards only the best and the brightest, according to this article.

10. Mr. Morita is satisfied with his company, and he will probably stay there all his working life.

7

Before you read, here are some questions to think about:

— Can you tell by the way a person stands or moves what country he or she is from?

— Do people from different countries and regions within a country use different gestures? Can you give some examples of these differences?

— We usually think of communication in terms of spoken language. What do you think *nonverbal communication* means?

— Have you ever watched television with the sound turned off? Were you able to understand anything about what was going on? If so, how?

San Sebastian, Spain. Children absorb body language along with spoken language.

HOW TO READ BODY LANGUAGE

1   All of us communicate with one another nonverbally, as well as with words. Most of the time we're not aware that we're doing it. We gesture with eyebrows or a hand, meet someone else's eyes and look away, shift positions in a chair. These actions we assume are random and incidental. But researchers have discovered in recent years that there is a system to them almost as consistent and comprehensible as language.

2   Every culture has its own body language, and children absorb its nuances along with spoken language. A Frenchman talks and moves in French. The way an Englishman crosses his legs is nothing like the way a male American does it. In talking, Americans are apt to end a statement with a droop of the head or hand, a lowering of the eyelids. They wind up a question with a lift of the hand, a tilt of the chin, or a widening of the eyes. With a future-tense verb they often gesture with a forward movement.

3   There are regional idioms, too: an expert can sometimes pick out a native of Wisconsin just by the way he uses his eyebrows during conversation. Your sex, ethnic background, social class, and personal style all influence your body language. Nevertheless, you move and gesture within the American idiom.

4   The person who is truly bilingual is also bilingual in body language. New York's famous mayor, Fiorello La Guardia, politicked in English, Italian, and Yiddish. When films of his speeches are run without sound, it's not too difficult to identify from his gestures the language he was speaking. One of the reasons English-dubbed foreign films often seem flat is that the gestures don't match the language.

5   Usually the wordless communication acts to qualify the words. What the nonverbal elements express very often, and very efficiently, is the emotional side of the message. When a person feels liked or disliked, often it's a case of "not what he said but the way he said it." Psychologist Albert Mehrabian has devised this formula: total impact of a message = 7 percent verbal + 38 percent vocal + 55 percent facial. The importance of the voice can be seen when you consider that even the words "I hate you" can be made to sound sexy.

6   Experts in kinesics—the study of communication through body movement—are not prepared to spell out a precise vocabulary of gestures. When an American rubs his nose, it may mean he is disagreeing with someone or rejecting something. But there are other possible interpretations, too. For example, when a student in conversation with a professor holds the older man's eyes a little longer than is usual, it can be a sign of respect and affection; it can be a subtle challenge to the professor's authority; or it can be something else entirely. The expert looks for patterns in the context, not for an isolated meaningful gesture.

7   Kinesics is a young science—developed in the 1950s—and very much the brainchild of one man, anthropologist Dr. Ray L. Birdwhistell. But it already offers a wide variety of small observations. (For example, eyebrows have a repertoire of about 23 possible positions; men use their eyebrows more than women do.) Most people find they can shut out conversation and concentrate on watching body language for only about 30 seconds at a time. Anyone can experiment with it, however, simply by turning on the television picture without the sound.

8   One of the most potent elements in body language is eye behavior. Americans are careful about how and when they meet one another's eyes. In our normal conversation, each eye contact lasts only about a second before one or both individuals look away. When two Americans look searchingly into each other's eyes, emotions are heightened and the relationship becomes more intimate. Therefore we carefully avoid this, except in appropriate circumstances.

9   Americans abroad sometimes find local eye behavior hard to interpret. "Tel Aviv was disturbing," one man recalled. "People stared right at me on the street; they looked me up and down. I kept wondering if I was uncombed or unzipped. Finally, a friend explained that Israelis think nothing of staring at others on the street."

10   Proper street behavior in the United States requires a nice balance of attention and inattention. You are supposed to look at a passerby just enough to show that you're aware of his presence. If you look too little, you appear haughty or secretive; too much, and you're inquisitive. Usually what happens is that people eye each other until they are about eight feet apart, at which point both cast down their eyes. Sociologist Dr. Erving Goffman describes this as "a kind of dimming of lights." In parts of the Far East it is impolite to look at the other person at all during conversation. In England the polite listener stares at the speaker attentively and blinks his eyes occasionally as a sign of interest. That eye-blink says nothing to Americans, who expect the listener to nod or to murmur something—such as "mm-hmm."

11   There are times when what a person says with his body gives the lie to what he is saying with his tongue. Sigmund Freud once wrote: "No mortal can keep a secret. If his lips are silent, he chatters with his fingertips; betrayal oozes out of him at every pore."

12   Thus, a man may successfully control his face, and appear calm and self-controlled—unaware that signs of tension and anxiety are leaking out, that his foot is beating on the floor constantly, restlessly, as if it had a life of its own. Rage is another emotion feet and legs may reveal. During arguments the feet often become tense. Fear sometimes produces barely perceptible running motions, a kind of nervous leg jiggle. Then there are the subtle, provocative leg gestures that women use, consciously and unconsciously.

13   Recent studies by psychologists suggest that posture often reflects a person's attitude toward people he is with. One experiment indicates that when men are with other men they dislike, they relax either very little or very much—depending on whether they see the other man as threatening. Women in this experiment always signaled dislike with very relaxed posture. And men, paired with women they disliked, were never tense enough about it to sit up rigidly.

14   Postures sometimes offer a guide to broad relationships within a group. Imagine that at a party, guests have been fired up by an argument. You may be able to spot at a glance the two sides of the argument by postures adopted. More of the pros, for example, may sit with crossed knees, the cons with legs stretched out and arms folded. A few middle-of-the-roaders may try a little of each—crossing their knees *and* folding their arms. If an individual abruptly shifts his body around in his chair, it may mean that he disagrees with the speaker or even that he is changing sides. None of this, of course, represents an infallible guide, but it is apparently significant enough to be worth watching for.

15   While children learn spoken and body language—proper postures, eye behaviors, etc.—they also learn a subtler thing: how to react to space around them. Man walks around inside a kind of private bubble, which represents the amount of air space he feels he must have between himself and other people. Anthropologists, working with cameras, have recorded the tremors and minute eye movements that betray the moment the individual's bubble is breached. As adults, however, we hide our feelings behind a screen of polite words.

16   Anthropologist Dr. Edward T. Hall points out that, for two unacquainted adult male North Americans, the comfortable distance to stand for private conversation is from arm's length to about four feet apart. The South American likes to stand much closer, which creates

problems when the two meet face to face. For, as the South American moves in, the North American feels he's being pushy; and as the North American backs off, the South American thinks he's being standoffish.

17   The American and the Arab are even less compatible in their space habits. Arabs like close contact. In some instances, they stand very close together to talk, staring intently into each other's eyes and breathing into each other's face. These are actions the American may associate with sexual intimacy and he may find it disturbing to be subjected to them in a nonsexual context.

18   The amount of space a man needs is also influenced by his personality—introverts, for example, seem to need more elbow room than extroverts. Situation and mood also affect distance. Moviegoers waiting in line to see a sexy film will line up much more densely than those waiting to see a family-entertainment movie.

19   George du Maurier once wrote: "Language is a poor thing. You fill your lungs with wind and shake a little slit in your throat and make mouths, and that shakes the air; and the air shakes a pair of little drums in my head . . . and my brain seizes your meaning in the rough. What a roundabout way and what a waste of time!"

20   Communication between human beings would be just that dull if it were all done with words. But actually, words are often the smallest part of it.

TURN TO COMPREHENSION CHECK AT END OF CHAPTER

1496 words

READING TIMES:
1st reading _____ minutes
2nd reading _____ minutes

READING SPEED:
8 minutes = 187 wpm
7 minutes = 214 wpm
6 minutes = 249 wpm
5 minutes = 299 wpm
4 minutes = 374 wpm

A. Analysis of Ideas and Relationships: Circle the letter next to the best answer.

1. The main idea of this article is that:
   a. people from different cultures have different space requirements.
   b. kinesics is a new science.
   c. body movements are as important as words in communication.

   Please explain your answer.

2. Put the following statements into logical order. Then refer to paragraph 1 to check your work.
   a. "We gesture with eyebrows or a hand, meet someone else's eyes and look away, shift positions in a chair."
   b. "These actions we assume are random and incidental."
   c. "All of us communicate with one another nonverbally, as well as with words."
   d. "But researchers have discovered in recent years that there is a system to them almost as consistent and comprehensible as language."

3. The main idea of paragraphs 2, 3, and 4 is that:
   a. body language differs in each culture.
   b. it is difficult to dub a foreign film into English.
   c. Americans communicate differently from Frenchmen.

   Please explain your answer.

4. In paragraph 6, sentence 2 is:
   a. the main idea of the paragraph.
   b. an example supporting the main idea.
   c. the conclusion of the paragraph.

5. According to paragraph 8, if you wanted to make an American feel uncomfortable, you could:
   a. interpret his eye behavior.
   b. stare into his eyes for one second.
   c. stare into his eyes for a long time.

6. In paragraphs 11 and 12, it appears that:
   a. it is difficult for a person to completely hide his emotions.
   b. if a person is tense, his foot will beat the floor restlessly.
   c. a person can manage to hide his emotions completely if he tries hard enough.

   Please explain your answer.

7. The subject of paragraphs 15, 16, 17, and 18 is:
   a. space requirements.
   b. cultural differences.
   c. personality differences.

   Please explain your answer.

8. The main idea of paragraph 17 is that:
   a. Americans and Arabs have different space requirements.
   b. Arabs like close contact.
   c. Americans are disturbed by close contact.

9. The author's attitude toward George du Maurier's description of language in paragraph 19:
   a. is not evident.
   b. is one of agreement.
   c. is one of disagreement.

   Why did you choose your answer?

10. You would be most likely to find the subject of body language discussed in:
    a. a history book.
    b. a sociology book.
    c. an English literature textbook.

B. **Interpretation of Words and Phrases: Circle the letter next to the best answer.**

1. "They **wind up** a question with a lift of the hand...."
   a. end
   b. blow away
   c. start

2. "... an expert can sometimes **pick out** a native of Wisconsin just by the way he uses his eyebrows...."
   a. pull out
   b. give
   c. identify

3. "Experts ... are not prepared to **spell out** a precise vocabulary of gestures."
   a. describe exactly
   b. give a hint about
   c. spell the words of

4. "Therefore, we carefully **avoid** this, except in appropriate circumstances."
   a. get rid of
   b. get around
   c. get along with

5. "... **he chatters with his fingertips** ..." (paragraph 11) means:
   a. he uses hand language.
   b. he taps his fingers nervously.
   c. he waves his fingers around.

6. "Imagine that at a party, guests have been **fired up** by an argument."
   a. hot
   b. attacked
   c. excited

7. "Most of the **pros,** for example, may sit with crossed knees, the **cons** with legs stretched out and arms folded."

   pros refers to:
   a. professionals
   b. very talented people
   c. those in favor of something

   cons refers to:
   a. those against something
   b. convicts
   c. untalented people

8. "Anthropologists, working with cameras, have recorded ... **minute** eye movements . . . ." Using your dictionary, answer the following questions.
   minute means:
   a. measurement
   b. 60 seconds
   c. very small

   The correct accent and pronunciation of this meaning is:
   a. min'ute (MIN'it)
   b. mi-nute' (mai-NYUT')

9. Dr. Hall **points out** that the proper distance to stand is about four feet apart.
   a. denies
   b. indicates
   c. guesses

10. ". . . as the North American **backs off,** the South American thinks he's being standoffish."
    a. retreats
    b. shouts
    c. touches his back

C. Synonyms: From this list choose a synonym for the word in bold type in each sentence. Be sure to use correct verb tenses and singular or plural forms for nouns.

to agree with	to suppose
anger	space (around a person)
arrogant	to have no pattern
curious	very delicate shades of meaning
powerful	very tense

1. We **assume** that other people understand us from our words.

2. We may think our gestures **are random.**

3. Your body language **is consistent with** the body language of other people in your culture.

4. Body language is not easy to comprehend because it is full of **nuance.**

5. Certain gestures have a very **potent** meaning in a culture.

6. What kinds of eye behavior are considered **haughty** in your culture?

7. If someone has an **inquisitive** look, he is probably interested in the topic.

8. Even if you try to keep your **rage** under control, your body will show it.

9. When I feel **nervous,** I jiggle my foot.

10. Some people require more **elbow room** than others do.

D. Prepositions and Verb-Completers: Write any appropriate preposition or verb-completer in the blank spaces.

1. We gesture _____ our eyebrows or hands, meet someone's eyes and then look _____ , or shift positions _____ a chair.

2. Americans are apt _____ end a statement _____ a lowering _____ the eyelids.

3. Experts _____ kinesics, the study _____ communication _____ body movement, are not prepared _____ spell _____ a precise vocabulary _____ gestures.

4. _____ parts of the Far East, it is impolite _____ look _____ the other person _____ all _____ conversation.

5. Signs _____ tension and anxiety always leak _____ .

6. Recent studies _____ psychologists suggest that posture often reflects a person's attitude _____ the people he is _____ .

7. Man walks _____ inside a kind _____ private bubble which represents the amount _____ air space he feels he must have _____ himself and others.

8. We hide our feelings _____ a screen _____ polite words.

9. _____ some instances, they stand very close together _____ talk, staring intently _____ each other's eyes and breathing _____ each other's faces.

10. The amount _____ space a man needs is also influenced _____ his personality.

E. Participles: Participles can be used as adjectives. The present participle replaces active verbs. The past participle refers to an act that has already affected a person or thing. In the following sentences, choose the appropriate participial form of the verb. Then find all the examples of participles used as adjectives in paragraphs 13 through 18 of Body Language.

1. relax:

   a. Music relaxes me. I like to listen to *relaxing* music at night.

   b. My father became relaxed during his vacation. He had a very *relaxed* appearance.

2. freeze:
   a. I buy food which has been frozen. I buy _____ food.
   b. The temperature is extremely cold today. It's _____ weather.

3. excite:
   a. The mystery story was so exciting that I stayed up all night to read it. It was an _____ story.
   b. The children waited excitedly for their grandparents to arrive. They were _____ children.

4. speak:
   a. English is spoken here. Can you understand _____ English well?
   b. Dogs can't speak. If I had a _____ dog, I could become rich!

5. absorb:
   a. That towel absorbs moisture well. Its special _____ power will clean up the spilled liquid quickly.
   b. Water can be absorbed into clothes. During the rainy season, the _____ moisture may ruin your clothes.

6. identify: Real money has special _____ marks to distinguish it from counterfeit money.

7. disturb:
   a. My friend's illness was a very _____ event for me.
   b. The _____ man shouted and screamed.

8. adopt: The _____ child was happy in her new home.

9. require: Is English a _____ subject in your school?

10. isolate: I lived in a very _____ location for several months. My nearest neighbor was 2 miles away.

Participles are also used in adjective phrases which are placed *after* the nouns they modify. Find examples of this usage in paragraphs 13 through 18 and then complete these sentences.

11. **relax:**

   a. The girl _relaxing_ on the park bench is my sister.

   b. The insomniac, _relaxed_ by a hot bath, finally fell asleep.

12. **identify:** The person _____ by the police was wanted for robbery.

13. **disturb:** The people in the next apartment, _____ by our noisy party, asked us to be more quiet.

14. **wait:** The children _____ to see the doctor seemed frightened.

15. **like:** The man, _____ by all, was elected mayor.

16. **produce:** Wine _____ in France is well known all over the world.

17. **relate:** I gave my cousin a book _____ to American history.

18. **behave:** The child, _____ very badly, was sent to bed early.

19. **vary:** The men and women, _____ in age from 25 to 60, are taking an exercise class together.

20. **make:** I like to wear clothes _____ by hand.

F. **Special Expressions: From this list choose the correct meaning for each of the expressions in bold type. Change the structure of the sentences, if necessary, to make the expression fit.**

brilliant idea	to look into (someone's) eyes quickly
to contradict	moderate
in general	to stare at (a person) intently
indirect	to study (someone) carefully
to know immediately	to treat casually

1. After the child broke the lamp, he **met his mother's eyes** but then looked away guiltily.

2. He **held my eyes** while I explained the problem.

3. The new theory is the **brainchild** of Dr. Birdwhistell.

4. During the job interview, the manager **looked me up and down.**

5. Israelis **think nothing of** staring at people on the street.

6. Although she says she is happy, her sad eyes **give the lie to** her smile.

7. Some people can **spot at a glance** when you are telling a lie.

8. According to that survey, most Americans are **middle-of-the-roaders.**

9. This outline will tell you **in the rough** all you need to know.

10. In a very **roundabout** way, we make our messages clear.

G. **Word Forms: Choose the correct word form to fit into each sentence. Use appropriate verb tenses, singular or plural forms for nouns, and passive voice where necessary.**

Noun	Verb	Adjective	Adverb
absorption	to absorb	absorbing absorbent	
disturbance	to disturb	disturbing disturbed	disturbingly
identification	to identify	identifying identifiable	
indication indicator	to indicate	indicative	
intention	to intend	intentional intent	intentionally intently
observation observer	to observe	observant	
politics politician		political	politically
requirement	to require	required	
success	to succeed	successful	successfully
tension	to tense	tense	tensely

1. **absorption, to absorb, absorbing, absorbent**
   a. That kind of cloth doesn't _____ moisture, so it's good for raincoats.
   b. This is such an _____ book that I can't put it down.
   c. A good sponge should be very _____ .
   d. The _____ of moisture by the soil is important for plant growth.

2. **politics, politician, political, politically**
   a. The _____ gave a speech at the local _____ club.
   b. Don't talk to me about _____ unless you have lots of information.
   c. _____ , I'm a middle-of-the-road voter.

3. **identification, to identify, identifying, identifiable**
   a. You should always carry some kind of _____ with you.
   b. That man has several _____ marks on his arm from being burned.
   c. Could you _____ that man if you saw him again?
   d. The man is easily _____ because he is unusually tall.

4. **observation, observer, to observe, observant**
   a. Have you ever _____ how other people's behavior differs from yours?
   b. Sally notices everything because she is so _____ .
   c. That news article makes some good _____ about our culture.
   d. Were you a participant in the meeting or just an _____ ?

5. **disturbance, to disturb, disturbing, disturbed, disturbingly**
   a. The _____ child hadn't learned to talk yet even though he was five years old.
   b. This was a very _____ situation for his parents.
   c. Those people are creating a _____ in front of the Embassy Building.
   d. Don't _____ people who are thinking very hard.
   e. I had a _____ sad experience the other day—my friend's mother died and it was impossible to comfort him at all.

6. **requirement, to require, required**
   a. Did you buy the _____ textbook for that course?
   b. Every week my boss _____ us to hand in a progress report.
   c. What are the _____ for being promoted to a supervisor's position?

7. **success, to succeed, successful, successfully**
   a. I'm sure Mrs. Harris _____ in her plans to become a lawyer.
   b. She is always _____ at anything she tries.
   c. She _____ completed college in three years.
   d. She will be a _____ because she is so determined.

8. **tension, to tense, tense, tensely**
   a. After Mr. and Mrs Butler argued, they felt very _____ .
   b. Mrs. Butler looked at her husband _____ and left the room.
   c. Mr. Butler finally broke the _____ by apologizing for forgetting their anniversary.
   d. I _____ my muscles in order to lift the heavy suitcase.

9. indication, indicator, to indicate, indicative
   a. The teacher _____ which exercises we were to do.
   b. Being tired all the time is an _____ that you may be sick.
   c. Mr. Costa's ready smile is _____ of his cheerful personality.
   d. The _____ on the speedometer said that we were driving 65 miles per hour.

10. intention, to intend, intentional, intent, intentionally, intently
    a. Why did you eat those cookies? They _____ for the party.
    b. I didn't do that _____ . It was an accident.
    c. The men watched the ballgame so _____ that they didn't talk.
    d. They had _____ expressions on their faces while they watched.
    e. We have the _____ to visit Italy on our next vacation.
    f. Everyone was invited to Bob's party except Paula. Bob doesn't like her, so it must have been _____ .

H. **Sentence Construction: Use each group of words in the given order and form to make an original, meaningful sentence.**

1. according to, article, communicate, gestures, as well as

2. eye behavior, is, potent, body language

3. arguments, tension, which, may, revealed, barely perceptible, body

4. recent studies, psychologists, posture, indicative of, person's, toward

5. also, learn, react, space

I. **Topics for Discussion and Composition**

1. This article describes some typical body language used by Americans, Arabs, Israelis, and others. What are some typical types of body language used by people in your country or area of the country? Please give some examples to illustrate your answer.

2. This article states that body language varies from country to country and even from region to region within a single country. What differences have you noticed in various people's body language? (For example: gestures, facial expressions, keeping distance, embracing, shaking hands, eye behavior.)

3. Cultural differences also occur in the attitude of people toward time. For example, being "on time" is important in some countries, but in other

countries people are more casual about time. How do people in your native country feel about time? What significance do they give to lateness, punctuality, telling time, using watches and calendars, and store hours? Do you think people from urban areas are more time-conscious than people from rural areas? If so, why? If not, why not?

4. In your culture, does a person's sex make a difference in his or her use of body language? Discuss any differences that relate to casualness, politeness, space, gestures, or eye behavior. Are there other differences?

5. Study the photograph accompanying this article. What do you think is happening? Why? Compare your reactions to the photograph with the reactions of other people in your class.

6. Do you feel that Dr. Birdwhistell's theory is valid? Do you think that a science of kinesics really exists? Give several specific reasons for your position.

J. **Reading Reconstruction: Read this paragraph as many times as you can in three minutes. Then, with your book closed try to restate the ideas in writing as clearly and completely as you can. (See exercise J in Chapter 1 for complete instructions.)**

Space Requirements

How much living space does a person need? What happens when these space requirements are not adequately met? Sociologists and psychologists are conducting experiments on rats to try to determine the effects of overcrowding on humans. Recent studies have shown that the behavior of rats is greatly affected by space. If rats have adequate living space, they eat well, sleep well, and reproduce well. But if their living conditions become too crowded, their behavior patterns and even their health change perceptibly. They cannot sleep and eat well, and signs of fear and tension become obvious. The more crowded they are, the more they tend to bite each other and even kill each other. Thus, for rats, population and violence are directly related. Is this a natural law for human society as well? Is adequate space not only desirable but essential for human survival?

Key words (to be written on the chalkboard):

space	overcrowding	crowded	violence
requirements	behavior	tension	essential
experiment	adequate	population	survival
effects			

Comprehension Check

On a separate piece of paper, write the numbers 1 through 10 on both sides. Mark one side "Test 1" and the other side "Test 2." Read each statement and decide whether it is true or false. Write "T" after true statements and "F" after false statements under Test 1. After you have finished the comprehension check, turn Test 1 face down. Then read the article again and do the comprehension check again under Test 2. Base your answers on the information in this article *only*, even if you disagree with what the author said.

1. According to this article, facial expressions and body movements are as important as words in communication.

2. The person most responsible for kinesics—the study of communication through body movement—was Sigmund Freud.

3. Men use their eyebrows more than women do.

4. In a normal conversation between Americans, eye contact lasts about 4 seconds before one or both individuals look away.

5. According to this article, in certain parts of the Far East, people watch each other attentively during a polite conversation.

6. Americans and Englishmen act differently when they are listening attentively to another person.

7. According to this article, when a woman is with someone she does not like, she always assumes a very relaxed posture.

8. When a man is with a man he does not like, he sometimes assumes a very relaxed posture.

9. South Americans and Arabs are more similar in their space requirements than North Americans and Arabs are.

10. A very aggressive, outgoing person needs less space than a passive, introverted person.

8

Before you read, here are some questions to think about:

— Have you ever met a super salesperson, someone who could sell you anything?

— Why was this person so successful in selling?

— Have you ever bought something you didn't really want and definitely didn't need? Why did you buy it?

— What are the selling techniques that convince us to buy—even when we don't really want or need what we are buying?

TO TRUST, PERCHANCE TO BUY

[The author, Donald J. Moine, has a Ph.D. in Psychology from the University of Ontario, where he conducted a study of salespeople in various fields. Dr. Moine found that the best salespeople use hypnosis techniques: they mirror the thoughts, tone of voice, speech tempo and mood of the customer—to persuade the customer to buy their product.]

Getting in Sync

1 The best salespeople first establish a mood of trust and rapport by means of "hypnotic pacing"—statements and gestures that play back a customer's observations, experience, or behavior. Pacing is a kind of mirror-like matching, a way of suggesting: "I am like you. We are in sync. You can trust me."

2 The simplest form of pacing is "descriptive pacing," in which the seller formulates accurate, if banal, descriptions of the customer's experience. "It's been awfully hot these last few days, hasn't it?" "You said you were going to graduate in June." These statements serve the purpose of establishing agreement and developing an unconscious affinity between seller and customer. In clinical hypnosis, the hypnotist might make comparable pacing statements. "You are here today to see me for hypnosis." "You told me over the phone about a problem that concerns you." Sales agents with only average success tend to jump immediately into their memorized sales pitches or to hit the customer with a barrage of questions. Neglecting to pace the customer, the mediocre sales agent creates no common ground on which to build trust.

3 A second type of hypnotic pacing statement is the "objection pacing" comment. A customer objects or resists, and the sales agent agrees, matching his or her remarks to the remarks of the customer. A superior insurance agent might agree that "insurance is not the best investment out there," just as a clinical hypnotist might tell a difficult subject, "You are resisting going into trance. That's good. I encourage that." The customer, pushing against a wall, finds that the wall has disappeared. The agent, having confirmed the customer's objection, then leads the customer to a position that negates or undermines the

objection. The insurance salesperson who agreed that "insurance is not the best investment out there" went on to tell his customer, "but it does have a few uses." He then described all the benefits of life insurance. Mediocre salespeople generally respond to resistance head-on, with arguments that presumably answer the customer's objection. This response often leads the customer to dig in his heels all the harder.

4   The most powerful forms of pacing have more to do with how something is said than with what is said. The good salesperson has an ability to pace the language and thought of any customer. With hypnotic effect, the agent matches the voice tone, rhythm, volume, and speech rate of the customer. He matches the customer's posture, body language, and mood. He adopts the characteristic verbal language of the customer ("sounds good," "rings a bell," "get a grip on"). If the customer is slightly depressed, the agent shares that feeling and acknowledges that he has been feeling "a little down" lately. In essence, the top sales producer becomes a sophisticated biofeedback mechanism, sharing and reflecting the customer's reality—even to the point of breathing in and out with the customer.

5   I have found only one area in which the top salespeople do not regularly pace their customers' behavior and attitudes—the area of beliefs and values. For example, if a customer shows up on a car lot and explains that she is a Republican, a moderately successful salesman is likely to say that he is too, even if he isn't. The best salespeople, even if they are Republicans, are unlikely to say so, perhaps because they understand that "talk is cheap" and recognize intuitively that there are deeper, more binding ways of "getting in sync" with the customer.

The Soft Sell

6   Only after they have created a bond of trust and rapport do the top salespeople begin to add the suggestions and indirect commands that they hope will lead the customer to buy. One such soft-sell technique is using their patently true pacing statements as bridges to introduce influencing statements that lead to a desired response or action. For example: "You are looking at this car, and you can remember the joy of owning a new reliable car," or "You are 27 years old, and we figure that your need for life insurance is $50,000." These pacing and leading statements resemble the way a hypnotist leads a client into hypnosis: "You are sitting in this chair, and you are listening to my voice"—the unarguable pacing statements—"and your eyelids are getting heavy, and they are beginning to close."

7   There does not have to be any logical connection between the pacing statement and the leading statement. They can be totally unrelated; yet when they are connected linguistically, they form a "sales

logic" that can be powerfully effective, even with such presumably analytic and thoughtful customers as doctors and college professors.

8   The power of these leading statements comes from the fact that they capitalize on the affirmative mental state built by the undeniably true pacing statements with which the customer is now familiar. Customers who have agreed with salespeople expect, unconsciously, further agreement, just as customers who have disagreed expect further disagreement. The "traditional" truth of these pacing statements rubs off on the leading statements, and, without knowing it, the customer begins to take more and more of what the sales agent says as both factual and personally significant. Using hypnotic language, the agent activates the customer's desire for the product.

9   Average sellers combine pacing and leading statements less frequently and with less skill than do their superior colleagues. They also speak in shorter, choppier sentences, and thus fail to create the emotional web of statements in which the truthful and the possible seem to merge.

10   One of the most subtle soft-sell techniques is to embed a command into a statement. "A smart investor knows how to *make a quick decision, Robert.*" "I'm going to show you a product that will help you, *Jim, save money.*" Salespeople ensure that their embedded commands come across by changing the tone, rhythm, and volume of their speech. Typically, as they pronounce the commands, they intuitively slow their speech, look the customer directly in the eyes, and say each word forcefully. A clinical hypnotist does the same thing deliberately. "If you will *listen to the sound of my voice*, you will be able to relax."

11   The placement of an individual's name in a sentence seems like a trivial matter; yet the position of a name can make a significant difference in how strongly the sentence influences the listener. Placed before or after the command portion of a sentence, it gives the command an extra power.

12   By changing their speech rate, volume, and tone, the best sales agents are able to give certain phrases the effect of commands. "If you can *imagine yourself owning this beautiful car and imagine how happy it will make you*, you will want to, *Mr. Benson, buy this car.*" The two phrases beginning with "imagine" become commands for the customer to do just that. Owning the car is linked to the leading statement of how happy it will make the customer. Finally, the statement carries the embedded command: "*Mr. Benson, buy this car.*"

TURN TO COMPREHENSION CHECK AT END OF CHAPTER

1200 words

READING TIMES:	READING SPEED:
1st reading _____ minutes	10 minutes = 120 wpm
2nd reading_____ minutes	8 minutes = 150 wpm
	6 minutes = 200 wpm
	4 minutes = 300 wpm

A. **Analysis of Ideas and Relationships: Circle the letter next to the best answer.**

1. The main point of this article is that:
   a. the most successful salespeople use a lot of hypnosis techniques.
   b. salespeople should study hypnosis to improve their sales skills.
   c. the best salespeople are unethical and will do anything to sell their products.

   Please explain your answer.

2. "The best salespeople first establish a mood of trust and rapport by means of 'hypnotic pacing'—statements and gestures that play back a customer's observations, experience, or behavior." What is **hypnotic pacing**?
   a. Statements and gestures that play back a customer's observations, experience, or behavior.
   b. A mood of trust and rapport.
   c. Observing the customer's behavior and gestures.

3. "The simplest form of pacing is 'descriptive pacing,' in which the seller formulates accurate, if banal, descriptions of the customer's experience. 'It's been awfully hot these last few days, hasn't it?'" How is the second sentence related to the first sentence?
   a. The second sentence is a general statement, and the first sentence is an example of descriptive pacing.
   b. The first sentence is a general statement, and the second sentence is an example of descriptive pacing.
   c. The first sentence introduces a topic, and the second sentence introduces a new topic.

   Please explain your answer.

4. In paragraph 2, sentence 4 ("These statements . . ."), **these statements** refers to:
   a. the previous sentence.
   b. the following two sentences.
   c. the previous two sentences.

5. In paragraph 2, the two sentences "You are here today to see me for hypnosis" and "You told me over the phone about a problem that concerns you" are examples of:
   a. hypnotic suggestions.
   b. the soft-sell technique.
   c. descriptive pacing.

6. Which statement is NOT necessarily true?
   a. The best salespeople mirror their customers' political and religious beliefs.
   b. The best salespeople pick up their customers' speech patterns and use them in their pacing statements.
   c. The best salespeople put subtle commands into their soft-sell statements.

7. According to paragraph 6, "You are 27 years old, and we figure your need for life insurance is $50,000."
   "**You are 27 years old**" is an example of:
   a. a pacing statement.
   b. a leading statement.

   "**we figure your need for life insurance is $50,000**" is an example of:
   a. a pacing statement.
   b. a leading statement.

8. The writer of this article suggests that:
   a. the best salespeople set up an atmosphere of agreement through their pacing statements, and this leads the customer unconsciously to expect that they will agree on other things as well.
   b. most customers, particularly well-educated customers, recognize soft-sell techniques, and they do not respond to them.
   c. the best salespeople do not use the customer's first name because they realize that people object to this form of intimacy.
   Explain your answer.

9. Which part of the statement "I'm going to show you a product that will help you, Jim, save money" is the embedded command?
   a. The whole statement.
   b. The last four words.
   c. The last three words.

10. In an embedded command, the customer's name is most effectively used:
    a. right before the command: **Jim, save money**.
    b. right after the command: **save money, Jim**.
    c. either right before or right after the command.

B. **Interpretation of Words and Phrases:** Circle the letter next to the best answer.

1. "We are in sync" is another way of saying:
   a. we are alike, particularly in our way of thinking.
   b. we are going to like each other.
   c. we don't have the same ideas, but we respect each other's ideas.

2. The best salespeople create **a common ground** upon which to build trust.
   a. a pleasant physical environment
   b. a friendly atmosphere
   c. an area of agreement

3. Mediocre salespeople **jump immediately into** their sales talk.
   a. move smoothly into
   b. rush too quickly into
   c. gradually begin

4. "... insurance is not the best investment **out there**."
   a. in that area of the country
   b. available
   c. at this time

5. The best salespeople do not respond to resistance from the customer **head-on**.
   a. directly
   b. indirectly
   c. precisely

6. If the sales agent argues with the customer over an objection, the customer often **digs in his heels all the harder.**
   a. forgets the objection and goes on to other matters
   b. sees that he was wrong to object and admits it
   c. objects even more strongly

7. What does it mean when someone says, "That rings a bell"?
   a. That sounds familiar to me.
   b. That is a good idea.
   c. That is a bad idea.

8. The salesman said, "These figures will help you **get a grip on** the efficiency of this car."
   a. hold on to
   b. pick up
   c. understand

9. What does the expression "talk is cheap" mean?
   a. It is not good to talk.
   b. Talk is better than action.
   c. Words without action don't mean much.

10. The truth of the pacing statements **rubs off on** the leading statements.
   a. does not influence or affect
   b. influences or affects
   c. is contradicted by

C. **Synonyms:** From this list choose a synonym for the word in bold type in each sentence. Use appropriate tenses for verbs and singular or plural forms for nouns.

a strong natural attraction	to mirror
it would appear that	persuasive sales talk
unoriginal and boring	average
gently persuasive selling techniques	to match
an atmosphere of trust	obviously

1. The best salespeople try to build **rapport** with their customers before they try to sell them anything.

2. They do this by making statements that **play back** the customers' observations and experience.

3. Sometimes they start off by making accurate but **banal** statements about the weather, for example.

4. The best salespeople try to create **an affinity** between the customers and themselves so the customers will trust them later on.

5. Only after establishing an atmosphere of trust do the best salespeople begin their **sales pitch**.

6. **Mediocre** salespeople, on the other hand, begin their sales pitch immediately, before trust has been established.

7. The best salespeople try **to pace** the language, speech, and body language of their customers.

8. They use **patently** true pacing statements ("What a beautiful sunny day") to introduce influencing statements ("A great day to buy a car, Janis").

9. They use **soft-sell techniques**, which are composed of influencing statements and indirect commands.

10. **Presumably** these hypnosis techniques work well in selling—because the best salespeople certainly sell much more than mediocre salespeople do.

D. Prepositions and Verb-Completers: Write any appropriate preposition or verb-completer in the blank spaces.

1. The best salespeople try _____ establish a feeling _____ trust _____ the beginning.

2. _____ contrast, mediocre salespeople go _____ their sales talk immediately _____ trying _____ establish this atmosphere _____ trust.

3. The best salespeople begin _____ making obvious comments _____ the weather, _____ example.

4. These pacing comments are a way _____ creating a feeling _____ common experience.

5. The best salespeople imitate the speech patterns and mannerisms _____ their customers.

6. They try _____ speak _____ the same speed and _____ use many _____ the same expressions.

7. Once they have established an atmosphere _____ rapport and trust, they begin _____ make influencing suggestions.

8. _____ example, they might say, "It's getting cold now, and you need _____ have a car you can really depend _____."

9. The customer becomes more and more influenced _____ these techniques _____ gentle persuasion.

10. The author _____ this article maintains that many _____ the most successful sales techniques are techniques _____ hypnosis.

E. Cloze Exercise: Select the best word to fill in each blank. Sometimes there may be more than one possible answer.

The best salespeople first establish a mood of trust and rapport by means of "hypnotic pacing"—statements and gestures that play back a customer's observations, experience, or behavior. Pacing is a kind of

(1) _____-like matching, a way of
   (descriptive—mirror—rank)

(2) _____: "I am like you. We (3) _____ in sync.
   (telling—asking—suggesting)   (run—live—are)

You can trust (4) _____." The simplest form of
              (yourself—me—people)

(5) _____ is "descriptive pacing," in which
(hypnosis—pacing—matching)

(6) _____ seller formulates accurate, if banal,
(a—the—this)

(7) _____ of the customer's experience. "It's
(conclusions—descriptions—evaluations)

(8) _____ awfully hot these last few (9) _____,
(getting—being—been)   (days—hours—minutes)

hasn't it?" "You said you (10) _____ going to graduate in June."
(are—were—was)

(11) _____ statements serve the purpose of
(This—The—These)

(12) _____ agreement and developing an
(making—persuading—establishing)

unconscious (13) _____ between seller and customer.
(thing—thought—affinity)

F. Super Sales Talk

1. Classify these statements as: a) pacing statement, b) influencing statement, or c) embedded command statement.

   The weather's been so cool the last few days, hasn't it? _____

   You owe it to yourself to buy a new dress, Christina. _____

   Your oldest daughter's already in college now, isn't she? _____

   Traffic is just terrible on Grand Street these days. Do you think they'll ever finish repairing those potholes? _____

   You'll love having a car you can depend on. _____

   You'll find that this microwave oven will, believe it or not, Marianne, save energy *and* money. _____

   For some reason, I've been feeling a little down lately, too. Maybe it's the after-holiday blues. _____

   Blue is certainly your color. _____

2. Write a short dialogue between a salesperson and a customer in which you try to use pacing statements, influencing statements, and embedded command statements such as the preceding ones.

   SP: Isn't it a lovely day today? It's just like summer, isn't it?
   C:

G. **Word Forms:** Choose the correct word form to fit into each sentence referring to the chart as necessary. Use appropriate verb tenses, singular or plural forms for nouns, and passive voice where necessary.

Noun	Verb	Adjective	Adverb
agreement	to agree	agreeable agreed	agreeably
commander command	to command	commanding	commandingly
comparison	to compare	comparable	comparably
hypnotist hypnosis	to hypnotize	hypnotic	hypnotically
investor investment	to invest		
logic		logical	logically
memory memorization	to memorize	memorized	
resister resistance	to resist	resistible irresistible	irresistibly
trustee trust	to trust	trusting trusted	trustingly
truth		true	truly

1. **trustee, trust, to trust, trusting, trusted, trustingly**
   a. Who is the _____ of that estate?
   b. She is a warm, _____ person.
   c. Can you _____ her with this information?
   d. Pick out your most _____ friend and discuss this matter with him or her.
   e. Friendship is built upon _____ .
   f. He looked at her _____ .

2. **hypnotist, hypnosis, to hypnotize, hypnotic, hypnotically**
   a. Would you like to be _____ ?
   b. His voice had a _____ quality to it.
   c. He kept repeating the same words and phrases _____ .
   d. Some doctors use _____ to relax their patients.
   e. Would you ever go to a _____ ?

3. **comparison, to compare, comparable, comparably**
   a. These two products are _____ priced.
   b. I wish you wouldn't _____ me to him.
   c. There is no _____ between us.
   d. This model is _____ to that one in price.

4. **agreement, to agree, agreeable, agreed, agreeably**
   a. One reason he is such a good salesman is that he has a very _____ personality.
   b. Don't sign the _____ without reading the small print.
   c. I found myself _____ with everything she said.
   d. He reacted _____ .
   e. We were _____ that the conditions of the contract were fair and equitable.

5. **memory, memorization, to memorize, memorized**
   a. I have a very bad _____ .
   b. She has great powers of _____ .
   c. How long will it take you to _____ this speech?
   d. A _____ speech is sometimes rather boring to listen to.

6. **investor, investment, to invest**
   a. Land is a good _____ .
   b. Do you want to _____ some money in this land?
   c. How many _____ are there in that investment club?

7. **resister, resistance, to resist, resistible, irresistible, irresistibly**
   a. I am afraid that she was _____ attracted to him.
   b. I couldn't _____ laughing behind his back.
   c. In the 1960s, he was a war _____ .
   d. She thought she was _____ , but in fact she was quite _____ .
   e. He has no _____ to respiratory infections.

8. **logic, logical, logically**
   a. Let's look at the matter _____ .
   b. From the point of view of _____ , it doesn't make sense.
   c. She has a very _____ mind.

9. **truth, true, truly**
   a. Is what he says really _____ ?
   b. Go ahead and tell me the whole _____ .
   c. It is _____ wonderful news!

10. **commander, command, to command, commanding, commandingly**
    a. Your wish is my _____ .
    b. He has a _____ presence.
    c. She spoke _____ .
    d. He _____ the troops to retreat.
    e. Who is the _____-in-chief?

H. **Sentence Paraphrase: Make new sentences using these sentence frames, and then make up your own sentences. You may add or leave out words, but try to retain the meaning of the original sentence.**

1. Only after they have created a bond of trust and rapport do the top salespeople begin to add the suggestions and indirect commands that they hope will lead the customer to buy.

   The top salespeople do not _____

   _____

   _____

   until they _____ .

   Other possible sentences:

2. The best salespeople, even if they are Republicans, are unlikely to say so.

   The best salespeople probably _____

   _____

   even if _____ .

   Other possible sentences:

3. Dr. Moine found that the best salespeople use hypnosis techniques.

   Hypnosis techniques _____

   _____ , according to _____

   _____ .

   Other possible sentences:

I.   **Topics for Discussion and Composition**

1. We have all been in the position of buying something we hadn't intended to buy. Sometimes it turns out to be a great mistake. But sometimes it turns out to be a good idea. Please describe a situation in which you bought something you hadn't intended to buy. Why did you buy it? What kind of sales pressure did you confront? Why was it useful to you later on?

2. We are all aware of the negative aspects of salespeople and selling. But what about the positives? What do skilled salespeople contribute? How can they help their customers to make better purchases? Give specific examples wherever possible.

3. Selling styles vary from culture to culture. In some cultures, the customer is under very little pressure to buy. The relationship between customer and seller is relatively calm and unemotional. In other cultures, there is a very intense relationship between customers and seller; the bargaining is heated and prolonged. Compare the selling style of your country with that of the U.S. (or another country, if you prefer). Which sales style do you prefer? Why? Which is more effective? Why? Give specific reasons and examples.

4. Have you ever worked as a sales agent or clerk? If so, describe the experience. Where did you work? What were you selling? Who were your customers? How did you approach them? How would you describe your selling style? What sales techniques seemed to be particularly effective? Why? Did you enjoy your sales experience? How did you feel when you sold something? Why? Would you do it again?

5. How do you think salespeople view customers? How do you think they categorize them? Do you think most salespeople respect their customers? Which ones do you think they respect most? Why? Which ones do they respect least? Why? Give specific reasons and examples.

J. Reading Reconstruction: Read this paragraph as many times as you can in three minutes. Then, with your book closed, try to restate the ideas in writing as clearly and completely as you can. (See exercise J in Chapter 1 for complete instructions.)

A Good, Used Car

He was an old man, and he was buying a car, not a new car but a good, used car. He thought he wanted a big car, big enough for his children and his grandchildren. He wanted to be able to take them for drives and to buy ice cream. The salesman, after talking to the old man for quite a while, realized that the old man's children and grandchildren didn't come to see him that often. They lived in another state, and he usually went to see them. The salesman also realized that the old man didn't really need a big car. In fact, it would be quite expensive and inconvenient for him. The salesman thought about the old man and his life, and he thought about his used cars. Suddenly he thought of the perfect solution: a medium-sized car in excellent condition. It wouldn't be too expensive to run, it would be reliable, and it would be big enough for four or five people. This car would be economical and dependable on the road, so the old man could drive to see his family if he wanted to. The salesman suggested that the old man consider this car, and he explained why he thought it would be a good car for him. The old man thought it over, and he took the salesman's advice. He liked the car, and he appreciated the fact that the salesman had understood his real needs—better than he himself had, as a matter of fact.

Key words (to be written on the chalkboard):

old man	inconvenient	economical	advice
used car	solution	dependable	appreciated
salesman	medium-sized	suggested	understood
realized	reliable	consider	real needs
expensive			

Comprehension Check

On a separate piece of paper, write the numbers 1 through 10 on both sides. Mark one side "Test 1" and the other side "Test 2." Read each statement and decide whether it is true or false. Write "T" after true statements and "F" after false statements under Test 1. After you have finished the comprehension check, turn Test 1 face down. Then read the article again and do the comprehension check again under Test 2. Base your answers on the information in this article *only,* even if you disagree with what the author said.

1. The best salespeople begin their sales talk immediately.

2. If the customer objects to the product or service, the best salespeople may begin by agreeing with the objection in part.

3. Mediocre (average) salespeople often argue with the customer when the customer makes an objection.

4. Mediocre salespeople use more techniques of hypnosis than the best salespeople do.

5. The best salespeople develop their own style, and they do not alter it for individual customers.

6. The best salespeople get the customer to agree with them about unimportant things (for example, the weather) before they begin making influencing suggestions.

7. The best salespeople are very sensitive to their customer's moods and mannerisms.

8. The best salespeople find out their customer's political beliefs, and they claim that they have the same beliefs whether they really do or not.

9. The best salespeople use some of their customer's expressions and speech mannerisms.

10. Selling and hypnosis are both forms of persuasion.

Review Examination II (Chapters 5, 6, 7, and 8)

A. Content Summary: Answer these questions and explain these statements. (20 points: 5 points each)

1. Before you try to find a job opening, what do you have to do first?

2. "You do not have to be the best or the brightest to share in the goodies." Relate Mr. Morita's life to this statement.

3. "The person who is truly bilingual is bilingual in body language too." Explain this statement.

4. Explain this title: "To Trust, Perchance to Buy."

B. Word Forms: Look at the first word in each line. Write the appropriate form of this word in the sentence that follows it. Be careful to use appropriate verb tenses, singular and plural forms for nouns, and passive voice where necessary. (40 points: 2 points each)

(Example)

hopeful   Is there any ___*hope*___ in this situation?

1. decide   When you are looking for a job, try to think and act _____ .

2. compete   There is a lot of _____ in the job market right now.

3. act   Pursue your job search _____ .

4. qualify   The best-_____ person doesn't always get the job.

5. suggest   Ask friends and acquaintances for advice and _____ .

6. philosophy   Mr. Morita looks at his life _____ .

7. qualitative   _____-control meetings are very important in Japan.

8. exciting   There is an atmosphere of _____ in some of these discussions.

9. participant   Workers _____ willingly and eagerly in these meetings.

10. prosper   Japan is experiencing great economic _____ .

11. success   A person who is _____ in learning to speak another language should learn the body language also.

12. require   Different languages _____ different gestures and facial expressions.

13. identity   You can _____ a culture by its body language.

14. **observer**   It is always interesting to _____ people from different cultures interacting with each other.

15. **absorb**   Body language is an _____ subject.

16. **hypnosis**   Super salespeople use techniques of _____.

17. **agreement**   They try to get their customers to _____ with them about small things at first.

18. **trusting**   Slowly they build an atmosphere of _____.

19. **logic**   Their statements develop their own _____ pattern.

20. **true**   The best salespeople are _____ masters of their art.

C.   **Cloze: Choose the most appropriate word for each blank. (10 points: 1 point each)**

Every culture has its own body language, and children absorb its nuances along with spoken language. A Frenchman talks and

(1) _____ in French. The way (2) _____ Englishman
    (talks—moves—acts)   (an—the—this)

crosses his legs (3) _____ nothing like the way (4) _____
                     (are—was—is)   (a—the—this)

male American does it. (5) _____ talking, Americans are apt
                           (In—For—After)

(6) _____ end a statement with (7) _____ droop of the head
    (to—too—two)   (a—the—this)

(8) _____ hand, a lowering of (9) _____ eyelids. They
    (or—and—to)   (the—these—those)

wind up (10) _____ question with a lift of the hand, a tilt of the chin or
            (a—this—the)

a widening of the eyes.

D. Composition: Write a composition about *one* of these topics. (30 points)

1. Compare the working life and attitudes toward work in Japan with the working life and attitudes toward work in your country. Use Mr. Morita as an example of a typical Japanese worker. Be sure to discuss the relationship between the worker and his or her company in both countries.

2. Did you ever have a misunderstanding with a person from another culture because of differences in body language? If so, discuss this misunderstanding. When did you become aware of the cultural differences involved in the misunderstanding? What, if any, were the consequences of this misunderstanding? What are your feelings about it now? Why?

3. Imagine that you are hiring someone for a job. Specify what the job is and what the requirements for this job are. Discuss the characteristics you would be looking for in a job applicant. If you had two people with similar training and experience, how would you choose between them? Why? Be as specific as possible. Give examples to demonstrate your ideas.

9

Before you read, here are some questions to think about:

- What is your first language?
- Is it related to any other languages? If so, which ones?
- How do you know your language is related to other languages?
- What does your language have in common with these other languages? Give examples of similarities.

Indo-European Alphabets

German

Gaelic

Greek

Russian

Serbian

Armenian

Persian

Hindi

INDO-EUROPEAN LANGUAGES

[Languages are divided into families. In other words, related languages come from a common origin. For example, many of the present-day languages in Europe, Asia, and America come from a single parent language, Indo-European. This article comes from a book entitled *The Languages of the World* by Kenneth Katzner published in 1975 by Funk & Wagnalls, New York, New York.]

1   The Indo-European family of languages is the world's largest, embracing most of the languages of Europe, America, and much of Asia. It includes the two great classical languages of antiquity, Latin and Greek; the Germanic languages such as English, German, Dutch, and Swedish; the Romance languages such as Italian, French, Spanish, and Portuguese; the Celtic languages such as Welsh and Gaelic; the Slavic languages such as Russian, Polish, Czech, and Serbo-Croatian; the Baltic languages, Lithuanian and Latvian; the Iranian languages such as Persian and Pashto; the Indic languages such as Sanskrit and Hindi; and other miscellaneous languages such as Albanian and Armenian. In Europe only Basque, Finnish, Estonian, Hungarian, Turkish, and a few languages of Russia are not of this family; the others have apparently all descended from an original parent tongue.

2   Who were the original Indo-Europeans and when and where did they live? Since they left no written documents, which are, after all, the basis of history, the answers to these questions can be best obtained by attempting to reconstruct their language. If we may assume that a word that is similar in most of the Indo-European languages designates a concept that existed in the original Indo-European society and that, on the other hand, a word that varies in most Indo-European languages designates a concept not discovered until later, we may then draw certain tentative conclusions. It would appear that the Indo-Europeans lived in a cold northern region; that it was not near the water, but among forests; that they raised such domestic animals as the sheep, the dog, the cow, and the horse; that among wild animals they knew the bear and the wolf; and that among metals they probably knew only copper. Many believe that it was the use of the horse and chariot that enabled them to overrun such an enormous expanse of territory.

3   The general consensus is that the original Indo-European civilization developed somewhere in eastern Europe about 3000 B.C. About 2500 B.C. it broke up; the people left their homeland and migrated in many different directions. Some moved into Greece, others made their way into Italy, others moved through Central Europe until they ultimately reached the British Isles. Another division headed northward into Russia, while still another branch crossed Iran and Afghanistan and eventually reached India. Wherever they settled, the Indo-Europeans appear to have overcome the local inhabitants and imposed their language upon them. One must conclude that they were a most remarkable people.

4   The possibility of so many languages having descended from a common ancestor was first suggested in 1786, though the similarity of Sanskrit and Italian was noted as early as the sixteenth century. By 1818 more than fifty separate languages were established as Indo-European; Albanian was added to the list in 1854 and Armenian in 1875. The total number of Indo-European speakers is about 1,875,000,000 people, approximately half the earth's total population.

5   The following table, giving the equivalents of six English words in numerous languages, will serve to illustrate the basic interrelation of the Indo-European languages.

Indo-European Languages

English	month	mother	new	night	nose	three
Welsh	mis	mam	newydd	nos	trwyn	tri
Gaelic	mí	máthair	nua	oíche	srón	trí
French	mois	mère	nouveau	nuit	nez	trois
Spanish	mes	madre	nuevo	noche	nariz	tres
Portuguese	mês	mãe	novo	noite	nariz	três
Italian	mese	madre	nuovo	notte	naso	tre
Latin	mensis	mater	novus	nox	nasus	tres
German	Monat	Mutter	neu	Nacht	Nase	drei
Dutch	maand	moeder	nieuw	nacht	neus	drie
Icelandic	mánuður	móðir	nýr	nótt	nef	þrír
Swedish	manad	moder	ny	natt	näsa	tre
Polish	miesiac	matka	nowy	noc	nos	trzy
Czech	měsíc	matka	nový	noc	nos	tri
Rumanian	lună	mamă	nou	noapte	nas	trei
Albanian	muaj	nënë	i ri	natë	hundë	tre, tri
Greek	men	meter	neos	nux	rhīs	treis
Russian	mesyats	mat'	novy	noch'	nos	tri
Lithuanian	menuo	motina	naujas	naktis	nosís	trys
Armenian	amis	mayr	nor	kisher	kit	yerek
Persian	māh	mādar	nau	shab	bini	se
Sanskrit	mās	matar	nava	nakt	nās	trayas

TURN TO COMPREHENSION CHECK AT END OF CHAPTER

750 words

READING TIMES:
1st reading _____ minutes
2nd reading _____ minutes

READING SPEED:
7 minutes = 107 wpm
6 minutes = 125 wpm
5 minutes = 150 wpm
4 minutes = 188 wpm

A. **Analysis of Ideas and Relationships: Circle the letter next to the best answer or supply the information as asked.**

1. This article is about:
   a. languages of the world.
   b. oriental languages.
   c. Indo-European languages.

2. Complete this diagram using information from this article:

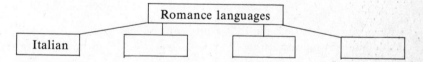

(*Note*: See the chart on page 155 for other Romance languages.)

3. Draw a circle around all of the *non*–Indo-European languages on this list:

Armenian	Estonian	Korean
Basque	French	Latvian
Chinese	German	Persian
Czech	Hungarian	Turkish
Dutch	Japanese	Welsh

4. English is related to **Germanic languages** in the same way as Persian is related to:
   a. Pashto.
   b. Iranian languages.
   c. Indo-Iranian languages.

5. Paragraph 2 explains how history can be reconstructed by:
   a. examining written reports and legal documents.
   b. examining linguistic (language) evidence: looking at the similarities and differences in the words of related languages.
   c. examining the themes of folktales and poetry.

6. If a number of related languages had many similar words for concepts such as **ice, snow,** and **cold** and relatively few words for **sand** and **heat,** one could assume that the speakers of the original parent language:
   a. preferred a cold climate to a warm climate.
   b. preferred a warm climate to a cold climate.
   c. lived in a cold climate.

7. "Wherever they settled, the Indo-Europeans appear to have overcome the local inhabitants and imposed their language upon them." The basis for this statement is:
   a. linguistic (language) evidence.
   b. legal documentation.
   c. the written records of the Indo-Europeans.

8. Put the following statements into logical order. Then refer to paragraph 3 to check your work.
   a. "The general consensus is that the original Indo-European civilization developed somewhere in eastern Europe about 3000 B.C."
   b. "Some moved into Greece, others made their way into Italy, others moved through Central Europe until they ultimately reached the British Isles."
   c. "About 2500 B.C. it broke up; the people left their homeland and migrated into many different directions."
   d. "Another division headed northward into Russia, while still another branch crossed Iran and Afghanistan and eventually reached India."

9. "Wherever **they** settled, the Indo-Europeans appear to have overcome the local inhabitants and imposed **their** language upon **them.**" Choose the correct answers for the words in bold type.

   They refers to: **Their** refers to: **Them** refers to:
   a. Indo-Europeans.   a. Indo-Europeans.   a. Indo-Europeans.
   b. local inhabitants.   b. local inhabitants.   b. local inhabitants.

10. Look at the word chart at the column beginning with **mother** and finish this sentence:
    In most Indo-European languages, the word for **mother** _____

    _____ .

B. **Interpretation of Words and Phrases: Circle the letter next to the best answer.**

1. "The Indo-European family of languages is the world's largest ...." This means that it is the world's largest:
   a. language.
   b. country.
   c. family of languages.

2. "In Europe only Basque, Finnish, Estonian, Hungarian, Turkish, and a few languages of Russia are not of this family ...."
   a. part of
   b. spoken in
   c. respected in

3. "... written documents, which are, **after all,** the basis of history."
   a. last but not least
   b. absolutely not
   c. all things considered

4. "... **on the other hand,** a word that varies in most Indo-European languages designates a concept not discovered until later ..."
   a. in contrast
   b. perhaps
   c. most likely

5. "... we may then draw certain tentative conclusions."
   a. We can be completely certain about our conclusions.
   b. We cannot come to any conclusions because the facts are too uncertain.
   c. We can come to possible but not definite conclusions.

6. "**It would appear that** the Indo-Europeans lived in a cold northern region ...."
   a. Definitely
   b. Probably
   c. Perhaps

7. "... among the wild animals they **knew** the bear and the wolf."
   a. were familiar with
   b. were introduced to
   c. had met

8. "**The general consensus is that** the original Indo-European civilization developed somewhere in eastern Europe about 3000 B.C."
   a. Most knowledgeable people agree that
   b. Some knowledgeable people agree that
   c. Most knowledgeable people disagree that

9. "... others **made their way into** Italy ...."
   a. worked to pay their way to
   b. traveled to
   c. returned to

10. "By 1818 more than fifty separate languages **were established as** Indo-European ...."
   a. claimed to be
   b. were developed to be
   c. were recognized as

C. **Synonyms: From this list choose a synonym for the word in bold type in each sentence. Use appropriate tenses for verbs and singular or plural forms for nouns.**

to differ	to include	to dominate
to get	to try	to end
to come from	to represent	agreement
to make it possible for		

1. The Indo-European family of languages **embraces** most of the languages of Europe, America, and much of Asia.

2. Linguists **have attempted** to reconstruct the original Indo-European language.

3. They **have obtained** information about the original Indo-European language by looking at existing languages.

4. If a word is similar in most Indo-European languages, it probably **designates** a concept that existed in the original Indo-European society.

5. On the other hand, if a word **varies** in most Indo-European languages, it probably designates a concept not discovered until later on.

6. The general **consensus** is that the original Indo-European civilization developed somewhere in eastern Europe about 3000 B.C.

7. About 2500 B.C., this civilization **broke up,** and the people traveled in all directions to new areas.

8. The use of the horse and chariot probably **enabled** the Indo-Europeans to overrun a great expanse of territory.

9. Wherever they settled, they **overran** the local inhabitants and imposed their language on them.

10. It is amazing to think that so many languages **descended from** a common ancestor.

D. Prepositions and Verb-Completers: Write any appropriate preposition or verb-completer in the blank spaces.

1. Most_____ the languages _____ Europe, America, and much _____ Asia belong_____ the Indo-European family_____ languages.

2. Many languages have descended _____ the original Indo-European language.

3. The Indo-Europeans probably lived _____ a cold northern region.

4. The original Indo-European civilization probably developed somewhere _____ eastern Europe.

5. _____ approximately 2500 B.C., the people left their homeland and migrated _____ many different directions.

6. They seem _____ have imposed their language _____ the existing population wherever they went.

7. Many people believe that the use _____ the horse and chariot enabled the Indo-Europeans _____ overrun such an enormous expanse _____ territory.

8. The original Indo-European civilization broke _____ about 2500 B.C.

9. Today the total number _____ Indo-European speakers is about 1,875,000,000 people.

10. Approximately half_____ the people _____ the world today speak Indo-European languages.

E. Cloze Exercise: Select the best word to fill in each blank. Sometimes there may be more than one possible answer.

Who were the original Indo-Europeans and when and where did they live? Since they left no __(1)_____ documents, which are, (written—spoken—legal) after __(2)_____, the basis of history, __(3)_____ (then—all—a while) (these—those—the) answers to these questions __(4)_____ be best obtained by (must—should—can) __(5)_____ to reconstruct their language. (attempting—trying—having) __(6)_____ we may assume that __(7)_____word that is (So—Whether—If) (a—this—the)

similar __(8)_____ most of the Indo-European
         (for—by—in)

(9)_____ designates a concept that
   (countries—populations—languages)

(10)_____ in the original Indo-European
    (happened—existed—was)

(11)_____ and   that,   on   the   (12)_____
    (society—place—country)   (other—same—second)

hand, a word that __(13)_____ in most Indo-European
                   (disappears—varies—remains)

languages __(14)_____ a concept not discovered
           (designates—is—makes)

(15)_____ later, we may then __(16)_____ certain
    (before—until—after)   (see—draw—think)

tentative conclusions.

F. **Language Study: Look at the Indo-European language family chart on page
    155 and answer these questions.**

1. English comes from the _____ branch of the _____ subgroup.

2. How many major languages are there in the Romance subgroup?_____

3. How many minor languages are there in the Indo-Iranian subgroup?
   _____

4. How many branches are there of the Slavic subgroup? _____

5. Irish and Scottish belong to the _____ branch of the _____
   subgroup.

6. Relationships:
   a. Germanic is related to Indo-European in the same way as Baltic is related
      to _____ .
   b. Hellenic is related to Greek in the same way as Italic is related to
      _____ .
   c. Welsh is related to Brythonic in the same way as Sanskrit is related to
      _____ .
   d. Iranian is related to Indo-Iranian in the same way as Southern is related
      to _____ .
   e. Western and Northern are related to Germanic in the same way as
      Eastern, Western, and Southern are related to _____ .

Indo-European Family

Family	Subgroup	Branch	Major Languages	Minor Languages
Indo-European	Germanic	Western	English, German, Yiddish, Dutch, Flemish, Afrikaans	Frisian, Luxembourgian
		Northern (Scandinavian)	Swedish, Danish, Norwegian, Icelandic	Faroese
	Italic		Latin	
	Romance		Italian, French, Spanish, Portuguese, Rumanian	Catalan, Provençal, Rhaeto-Romanic, Sardinian, Moldavian
	Celtic	Brythonic	Welsh, Breton	
		Goidelic	Irish (Gaelic), Scottish (Gaelic)	
	Hellenic		Greek	
			Albanian	
	Slavic	Eastern	Russian, Ukrainian, Belorussian	
		Western	Polish, Czech, Slovak	Sorbian (Lusatian)
		Southern	Bulgarian, Serbo-Croatian, Slovenian, Macedonian	
	Baltic		Lithuanian, Latvian (Lettish)	
			Armenian	
	Indo-Iranian	Iranian	Persian, Pashto, Kurdish, Baluchi, Tadzhik, Ossetian	
		Indic	Sanskrit, Hindi, Urdu, Bengali, Punjabi, Marathi, Gujarati, Bihari, Rajasthani, Oriya, Assamese, Kashmiri, Nepali, Sindhi, Sinhalese	Bhili, Romany, Maldivian

7. This table gives the translations of six words in six different languages. Which two languages appear to be unrelated to the others? (The two unrelated languages are non–Indo-European, and the others are Indo-European.) Explain why you picked these two languages. Do you know their names?*

a. month	mother	new	night	nose	three
b. mois	mère	nouveau	nuit	nez	trois
c. hilabethe	ama	berri	gai	südür	hirur
d. mês	mãe	novo	noite	nariz	três
e. lună	mamă	nou	noapte	nas	trei
f. hónap	anya	új	éjaszaka	orr	három

G. **Word Forms:** Choose the correct word form to fit into each sentence referring to the chart as necessary. Use appropriate verb tenses, singular or plural forms for nouns, and passive voice where necessary.

Noun	*Verb*	*Adjective*	*Adverb*
assumption	to assume		
basis	to base	basic	basically
concept conception misconception	to conceive to conceptualize		
conclusion	to conclude	concluding conclusive	conclusively
designation	to designate		
developer development	to develop	developing developed	
document documentation documentary	to document		

*a = English; b = French; c = Basque; d = Portuguese; e = Rumanian; f = Hungarian.

Noun	Verb	Adjective	Adverb
origin	to originate	original	originally
original			
originality			
remark	to remark	remarkable	remarkably
separation	to separate	separate	separately
		separated	

1. **origin, original, originality, to originate, original, originally**
   a. She was _____ from Vietnam.
   b. Can you tell if this is an _____ painting?
   c. I was impressed by the _____ of his ideas.
   d. This painting is definitely an _____ , and that one is definitely a fake.
   e. The Indo-European civilization _____ in approximately 3000 B.C. somewhere in eastern Europe.
   f. What is the _____ of that curious expression?

2. **document, documentation, documentary, to document**
   a. Is this the original _____ or is it a copy?
   b. Don't forget to _____ your sources in case your statements are questioned.
   c. He is a film-maker, and he makes _____ .
   d. Read this case and then check the _____ closely.

3. **basis, to base, basic, basically**
   a. What is the _____ for that statement?
   b. I _____ my argument on two points.
   c. We are in _____ agreement.
   d. _____ , I agree with you although I have one or two minor questions about your research methods.

4. **assumption, to assume**
   a. Don't make any hasty _____ .
   b. I _____ you are willing to take the risk.

5. **designation, to designate**
   a. She _____ me to represent her.
   b. The _____ of Martin Luther King's birthday as a legal holiday was a victory for Black Americans.

6. **concept, conception, misconception, to conceive, to conceptualize**
   a. Unfortunately, he couldn't_____ my plan, so he didn't recommend it to his boss.
   b. I think you have a basic _____ about the matter.
   c. This is not a new _____ , but it is interesting and useful.
   d. He couldn't _____ of who she was or what she was talking about.
   e. Do you have any _____ of how much that car would cost?

7. **conclusion, to conclude, concluding, conclusive, conclusively**
   a. Did you see the _____ of the movie?
   b. His research _____ proves that these two languages are related.
   c. What do you _____ from her strange behavior?
   d. The lawyer was presenting her _____ statements to the jury.
   e. The results of the tests were not _____ .

8. **developer, development, to develop, developing, developed**
   a. I don't know anything about the historical _____ of capitalism.
   b. & c. We must distinguish between_____ and_____ countries.
   d. Oh, I think he's a real estate _____ .
   e. Go on and _____ your argument fully.

9. **remark, to remark, remarkable, remarkably**
   a. What a curious _____ !
   b. She's a _____ person.
   c. These two houses are _____ similar.
   d. He _____ that the class was quite interesting.

10. **separation, to separate, separate, separated, separately**
    a. Did you hear that they filed for a legal _____ ?
    b. It may have been wise for them to _____ .
    c. They have _____ apartments, you know.
    d. They live _____ .
    e. The couple that was _____ argued all the time.

H. **Sentence Paraphrase: Make new sentences using these sentence frames, and then make up your own sentences. You may add or leave out words, but try to retain the meaning of the original sentence.**

1. The Indo-European family of languages is the world's largest, embracing most of the languages of Europe, America, and much of Asia.

    The world's largest _____

    Indo-European, which _____

    _____ .

    Other possible sentences:

2. Regarding the original Indo-Europeans, it would appear that they lived in a cold northern region, that it was not near the water, but among forests, and that they raised such domestic animals as the sheep, the dog, the cow, and the horse.

    The original Indo-Europeans probably _____

    _____

    _____ .

    They probably _____

    _____

    _____ .

    Other possible sentences:

3. The total number of Indo-European speakers is about 1,875,000,000 people, approximately half the earth's total population.

    About 1,875,000,000 people, approximately _____

    _____ ,

    speak _____ .

    Other possible sentences:

I.   Topics for Discussion and Composition

1. Many people believe that languages have different personalities. What do you think they mean? Compare your native language with English (or another language). How are they different in feeling?

2. Do you think that your language affects the way you see the world? If so, why do you think so? If not, why not? Give specific examples if you can.

3. How do you think language and culture are related? Can you really learn a language outside of the culture in which it is spoken? Use your own experience as an example if possible.

4. The world would be better off if there were only one language. Do you agree or disagree? Why? Give specific reasons and examples. Would you pick an existing language to be the single language? If so, why? Which one would you pick? If not, why not?

5. Language is power. Please explain this statement and give reasons and examples.

J.   Reading Reconstruction: Read this paragraph as many times as you can in three minutes. Then with your book closed, try to restate the ideas in writing as clearly and completely as you can. (See exercise J in Chapter 1 for complete instructions.)

The Origins of the Romance Languages

The Romance languages of today came originally from Latin, which was the official language of the Roman Empire. As the Empire spread gradually across a great part of Europe, Latin was introduced everywhere as the official language of government and administration. Spoken Latin was consistent from one area to another in the early days of the Empire. But later, when the Empire began to fall apart, the Roman administrators began to disappear. Gradually, the Latin of each region began to develop in its own way. Separated from each other by great distances and naturally influenced by the speech of the local people, each area slowly developed its own distinctive characteristics to the point where separate languages were formed. The modern Romance languages include the national languages: Italian, French, Spanish, Portuguese, and Rumanian. Catalan, Provençal, Rhaeto-Romanic, Sardinian, and Moldavian are regional Romance languages, limited in use to smaller areas within individual countries.

Key words (to be written on the chalkboard):

Romance languages	government	region
Latin	administration	distinctive
official	consistent	characteristics
Roman Empire	fall apart	separate
spread	Roman administrators	national
Europe	disappear	regional

Comprehension Check

On a separate piece of paper, write the numbers 1 through 10 on both sides. Mark one side "Test 1" and the other side "Test 2." Read each statement and decide whether it is true or false. Write "T" after true statements and "F" after false statements under Test 1. After you have finished the comprehension check, turn Test 1 face down. Then read the article again and do the comprehension check again under Test 2. Base your answers on the information in this article *only*, even if you disagree with what the author said.

1. The Indo-European language family is the largest language family in the world.

2. All present-day languages come from the Indo-European language.

3. Hungarian is not an Indo-European language.

4. The Indo-Europeans probably lived in a cold, northern area.

5. The Indo-Europeans were not familiar with horses.

6. The Indo-Europeans probably came from eastern Europe originally.

7. Their civilization developed around 3000 A.D.

8. The Indo-Europeans left their homeland after about 500 years.

9. They all went to western Europe.

10. More than one and a half billion people speak Indo-European languages today.

10

Before you read, here are some questions to think about:

— What is the role of grandmothers in the modern-day world?

— Do you think their role is changing? If so, why? If not, why not?

— What are the cultural expectations of grandmothers in your society? Are the expectations the same in all cultures?

— Do you think people recognize the needs of modern-day grandmothers? Are they sensitive to these needs? Why? Or why not?

FROM THE OTHER SIDE
OF THE GENERATION GAP

1   Contrary to the impression that grandmothers are delighted to help their grown daughters and care for their grandchildren, a study of multigenerational families indicates that many older women resent the frequent impositions of the younger generations on their time and energy.

2   "Young women with children are under a lot of pressure these days, and they expect their mothers to help them pick up the pieces," noted Dr. Bertram J. Cohler, a behavioral scientist at the University of Chicago. "This is often the strongest source of resentment on the part of Grandmother, who has finished with child caring and now has her own life to live. Grandmothers like to see their children and grandchildren, but on their own time."

3   Dr. Cohler is director of a study, sponsored by the National Institute on Aging, of 150 working-class families that live in a Midwestern suburb. He and a collaborator, Dr. Henry U. Grunebaum of Harvard Medical School, have already completed an intensive investigation of four such families in New England, summarizing their findings in a book, *Mothers, Grandmothers, and Daughters,* published recently by Wiley-Interscience for professional audiences.

4   Dr. Cohler tells of a middle-aged Boston woman who works as a seamstress all week and for her parish on Sundays. Every Saturday, her one day off, her daughter and family visit, expecting Mother to make lunch, shop, and visit. "That's not how she wants to grow old," said Dr. Cohler, who was told by the older woman: "My daughter would never speak to me if she knew how mad I get."

5   In all the four New England families studied, the older women resented the numerous phone calls and visits from their grown daughters, who often turned to their mothers for advice, physical resources, affection, and companionship as well as baby-sitting services. "American society keeps piling on the burdens for older people, particularly those in their 50s and 60s," Dr. Cohler said in an interview here. "They're still working and they're taking care of their grown children and maybe also their aged parents. Sometimes life gets to be too much. That's one reason many older folks move far away, to Florida or

Sun City [Arizona]. They need more space and time to attend to their own affairs and friends. Young people don't understand this, and that's part of what creates tension between generations."

6   He has found that, contrary to what the younger generations may think, older people have an enormous amount to do. "More than half of working-class grandmothers still work, and if they're retired they have activities in the community that keep them occupied," he said. "Each generation has got to appreciate the unique needs of the other," Dr. Cohler went on. "The younger generation has to realize that grandparents have busy, active lives and that they need privacy and more space for themselves. And the older generation has to realize that continuing to be part of the family is important to the younger generation and that they need help and support."

7   He noted that problems with interdependence between generations were likely to be more intense in working-class families than in middle and upper-class families. He explained that the working class tended to be geographically less mobile and to have fewer outside resources and that daughters were more likely to be reared with a strong family orientation and less emphasis on establishing an independent life.

8   Although the presumed disintegration of the extended family has received a lot of attention in recent years, Dr. Cohler maintains that there is more interaction between generations in families than ever before, particularly in cities, where job opportunities permit adults to remain where they grew up.

9   In only 10 percent of American families do grandparents live with their children and grandchildren, Dr. Cohler said, adding: "It's never been common to have three generations under one roof in America. That's part of the romance of the rural past, and it's a fiction. There's no evidence that the American family was once more extended and today is more nuclear."

10   "The American family is alive and well," he continued, citing his study. "Between the telephone, cars, and public transportation, there is a lot of communication and visiting back and forth between the generations." According to national survey data, more than half of those over age 65 visited with a younger member of the family within the last day and more than half the grandparents had seen a grandchild within the last week.

11   Dr. Cohler added that there were many attempts by the generations to influence each other. In the working-class families he and his colleagues have studied, the female members exert most of the influence. "Fathers and grandfathers are the least influential," he found. "Fathers

think they do a lot of influencing, but no one pays much attention to them." Enhancing the matrifocal tilt, as social scientists call it, is the tendency in working-class families for young married couples to move near where the wife's mother lives. Rather than resentment among the young husbands, the researchers found that they encouraged closeness with their wives' families and enjoyed it.

TURN TO COMPREHENSION CHECK AT END OF CHAPTER

852 words

READING TIMES:
1st reading _____ minutes
2nd reading_____ minutes

READING SPEED:
6 minutes = 142 wpm
5 minutes = 170 wpm
4 minutes = 213 wpm
3 minutes = 284 wpm

A. **Analysis of Ideas and Relationships: Circle the letter next to the best answer.**

1. **The generation gap** usually refers to the difference between young people and adults. The title of this article refers to:
   a. the gap between younger adults and older adults.
   b. the gap between young people and adults.
   c. the gap between men and women.

   Please explain your answer.

2. Paragraph 1:
   a. gives several examples of the generation gap.
   b. says that grandmothers are delighted to help their grown daughters.
   c. states the main idea of this article.

   Please explain your answer.

3. The last sentence in paragraph 4 implies **but does not directly say that:**
   a. the mother enjoys her daughter's visits every Saturday.
   b. the mother has not told her daughter that she doesn't like the Saturday visits.
   c. the mother does not want to grow old.

4. In paragraph 5, the third sentence ("They're still working..."):
   a. is not related to sentence 1.
   b. gives examples of sentence 1.
   c. is the main idea of the paragraph.

5. "Sometimes life gets to be too much." (paragraph 5)
   a. They enjoy their life very much.
   b. Sometimes life becomes very difficult.
   c. There are so many things to do that the grandparents can't decide.

6. "... the older generation has to realize that continuing to be part of the family is important to the younger generation and that **they** need help and support." **They** refers to:
   a. the younger generation.
   b. the older generation.
   c. the grandchildren.

7. According to the information in paragraph 7, which statement is **not** true?
   a. Daughters in working-class families try very hard to establish an independent life.
   b. Children of working-class families tend to stay in the same geographical area where they were raised.
   c. Interdependence between generations is more intense in working-class families.

   Please explain your answer.

8. Paragraphs 8, 9, and 10 discuss in general:
   a. the interaction between generations.
   b. the rural past.
   c. national survey data.

   Please explain your answer.

9. In paragraph 8, **maintains** means:
   a. takes care of.
   b. believes.
   c. disagrees.

10. According to paragraph 11, why are fathers and grandfathers the least influential?
   a. The article doesn't explain why.
   b. Because men don't spend much time with their families.
   c. Because young married couples move near where the wife's mother lives.

   Please explain your answer.

B. **Interpretation of Words and Phrases:** Circle the letter next to the best answer.

1. "... they expect their mothers to help them **pick up the pieces** ...."
    a. repair items that get broken
    b. pick up the children's clothing
    c. solve their problems

2. "This is often the strongest source of resentment **on the part of** Grandmother ...."
    a. against
    b. from
    c. in spite of

3. "Grandmothers like to see their children and grandchildren, **but on their own time.**"
    a. at any time
    b. when the children have time
    c. when the grandmothers have time

4. Saturday is her one **day off.**
    a. free day
    b. working day
    c. busy day

5. "Every Saturday, ... her daughter and family visit, expecting Mother to make lunch, shop, and visit. 'That's not how **she** wants to grow old.'" **She** refers to:
    a. granddaughter.
    b. daughter.
    c. grandmother.

6. "... the working class tended to **be geographically less mobile** ...."
    a. move from one part of the country to another frequently
    b. stay in one area and not move
    c. have fewer automobiles

7. "... there is more interaction between generations in families than ever before ...."
    a. There used to be more interaction.
    b. There is more interaction now.
    c. There has never been much interaction.

8. "**It's** never been common to have three generations under one roof in America."
    a. It has
    b. It was
    c. It is

9. "... there is a lot of communication and visiting back and forth ...."
   a. The parents always visit their children.
   b. The children always visit their parents.
   c. The parents and children visit each other.

10. "Rather than resentment among the young husbands, the researchers found that **they** encouraged closeness with their wives' families and enjoyed **it**."
    They refers to: **It** refers to:
    a. researchers.   a. closeness.
    b. husbands.   b. resentment.
    c. families.   c. wives.

C. **Synonyms: From this list choose a synonym for the word in bold type in each sentence. Be sure to use correct verb tenses and singular or plural forms for nouns.**

to add on	to increase	must
heavy responsibility	to lean	to show
idea	love	the opposite of
immense		

1. The mother's opinion was **contrary to** her daughter's.

2. Some young people have the **impression** that older people are not busy.

3. Recent studies **indicate** that older women resent the impositions on their time.

4. Daughters turn to their mothers for **affection** and companionship.

5. Society keeps **piling on** problems for older people.

6. It is quite a **burden** to work and care for aged parents.

7. We all have an **enormous** number of things to do.

8. You **have got to** understand that grandparents have busy, active lives.

9. The telephone and cars **have enhanced** communication between the generations.

10. Influence in the family **tilts** towards the mother.

D. Prepositions and Verb-Completers: Write any appropriate preposition or verb-completer in the blank spaces.

1. Contrary _____ the usual impression, many older women resent the impositions _____ the younger generation _____ their time and energy.

2. Women _____ children are under a lot _____ pressure.

3. Dr. Cohler is a behavioral scientist _____ the University _____ Chicago.

4. Dr. Cohler is the director _____ a study sponsored _____ the National Institute _____ Aging.

5. The older women resented the numerous visits _____ their grown daughters, who often turn _____ their mothers _____ advice.

6. That's part _____ what creates tension _____ generations.

7. The older generation has _____ realize that continuing _____ be part _____ the family is important _____ the younger generation.

8. Some daughters were reared _____ a strong family orientation and less emphasis _____ establishing an independent life.

9. Dr. Cohler maintains that there is more interaction _____ generations particularly _____ cities where job opportunities permit adults _____ remain where they grew _____ .

10. It's never been common _____ have three generations _____ one roof _____ America.

E. **Determiners: Write appropriate determiners in the blank spaces. If no determiner is necessary, write an "X" in the blank. (See Chapter 1 for complete instructions.)**

"_____ American family is alive and _____ well," he
        (1)   (2)
continued, citing _____ study. "Between _____ telephone,
                        (3)   (4)
cars, and public transportation, there is _____ lot of _____
                                                (5)   (6)
communication and visiting _____ back and forth between
                                (7)
_____ generations." According to national survey data, more than
    (8)
_____ half of those over _____ age 65 visited with _____
    (9)   (10)   (11)
younger member of _____ family within _____ last day and
                        (12)   (13)
more than _____ half _____ grandparents had seen
                (14)   (15)
_____ grandchild within _____ last week.
    (16)   (17)

F. **Antonyms: Each sentence contains two opposite words. Choose the word that completes the sentence correctly.**

1. (Take care of—Ignore) the cut on your finger, or else it will get infected.

2. The heat from the fire was so (intense—weak) that the firemen could not go near the building.

3. During the trial, it was difficult to explain how the man had stolen the car because there was (evidence—no proof).

4. I greatly (resent—appreciate) all your help. Thank you very much.

5. Don't talk to Mr. Bergen when he's (mad—happy). He'll just shout at you.

6. (Numerous—Very few) people can become multimillionaires.

7. When the child hurt herself, she (turned to—turned away from) her mother for comfort.

8. It would be wonderful if there were (tension—peace) all over the world.

9. During the week I eat (unique—ordinary) meals, but on the weekends I like to cook foods that are (unique—ordinary) to my native country.

10. As children grow up, they become more (dependent—independent) and make their own decisions.

H. **Sentence Construction: Use each group of words in the given order and form to make an original, meaningful sentence.**

1. young women, pressure, expect, help, pick up the pieces

2. older women, resented, visits, daughters

3. younger generation, realize, grandparents, active, and, privacy

4. communication, back and forth, generations

5. working-class families, female, exert, influence

I. **Topics for Discussion and Composition**

1. According to the study described in this article, grandmothers resent the frequent imposition of their daughters on their time and energy. Do you agree or disagree with this study? Explain your answer using several examples from your own experience or the experience of others.

2. What would a grandmother in your native country say if she read this article? Would she agree or disagree with it? Give several examples to explain your answer.

3. Do you think the problems of older people are different today than they were 50 or 100 years ago? Explain your answer using several examples.

4. What is the relationship between the old and the young in your native country?

5. How do you think you will want to live when you are old? Would you want to be near your children and grandchildren? Would you want to live independently? Give several examples to explain your answer.

6. How does the illustration reflect the points mentioned in the article?

J. **Reading Reconstruction: Read the paragraph on the next page as many times as you can in three minutes. Then, with your book closed, try to restate the ideas in writing as clearly and completely as you can. (See exercise J in Chapter 1 for complete instructions.)**

Grandparents and Grandchildren

Who needs grandparents? Children do. And their grandparents need them. Recent studies indicate that grandparents and grandchildren are better off when they spend large amounts of time together. What is the reason for this? Grandparents give children lots of affection with no strings attached, and the children make the grandparents feel loved and needed at a time when society may be telling the older people that they are a burden. Grandparents are a source of strength and wisdom and help ease the pressures between children and their parents.

Key words (to be written on the chalkboard):

needs	affection	burden
grandparents	no strings attached	strength
studies	loved	wisdom
indicate	needed	pressures

Comprehension Check

On a separate piece of paper, write the numbers 1 through 10 on both sides. Mark one side "Test 1" and the other side "Test 2." Read each statement and decide whether it is true or false. Write "T" after true statements and "F" after false statements under Test 1. After you have finished the comprehension check, turn Test 1 face down. Then read the article again and do the comprehension check again under Test 2. Base your answers on the information in this article *only*, even if you disagree with what the author said.

1. The study described in this article focused on working-class families.

2. Many of the older women resented the impositions on their time and energy.

3. According to the survey, grandmothers didn't like their grandchildren.

4. Many people in their 50s and 60s are not only working, but also taking care of their own aged parents.

5. Young people generally understand the problems of older people.

6. Grandparents have busy lives and need their own privacy.

7. Problems with interdependence are more intense in working-class families than in middle- and upper-class families.

8. Grandparents live with their children in only 10 percent of American families.

9. Less than 30 percent of grandparents see their grandchildren at least once a week.

10. Fathers have a lot of influence in working-class families.

11

Before you read, here are some questions to think about:

— What do you know about protein? How important is protein for maintaining health?

— What kinds of foods are rich in protein?

— Is it possible to get enough protein without eating meat, eggs, and milk?

— If you eat extra protein (more than your minimum daily requirement), will you be stronger?

PROTEIN: CAN YOU GET BY WITHOUT MEAT?

[This reading describes what protein is and how the human body must receive the protein it needs. It is taken from a report that examines how vegetarians should eat in order to get enough protein from their meatless diet. Although vegetarians eat no meat or fish, some vegetarians, called ovolacto-vegetarians, eat eggs and milk products. There will be several references in this reading to vegetarians and ovolacto-vegetarians.]

How much protein?

1 Protein has assumed an almost religious importance in the American diet. Some people still believe that eating protein makes you stronger and that strenuous exercise requires eating extra protein, though those notions were disproved long ago. Protein's primary function in the body is the creation and repair of tissue—from skin, muscles, and bones to hair and toenails. The amount of protein you need, therefore, depends more on your size and age than on your activity.

2 An average man's Recommended Daily Allowance (RDA) for protein is 56 grams; a woman's is 44 grams. The RDA for children is proportionally more for their weight than the RDA for adults because children are growing. The following table shows how the RDAs change with age and sex:

	Age (years)	Protein RDA (grams)
Children	1–3	23
	4–6	30
	7–10	34
Females	11–18	46
	19+	44
Males	11–14	45
	15+	56

3 The RDAs for protein, as for other nutrients, are set high to allow for the range of individual needs and for a margin of safety against deficiency. Controlled studies have shown that men eating only 30 to 35 grams of protein a day lost no body protein. That amount would be

provided by as little as four ounces of Swiss cheese, tuna, or similar protein-rich food. The RDAs also allow for the different absorption rates of animal and plant protein. Besides eating enough protein, you have to eat enough high-quality protein. The quality of a protein is determined by its amino acids.

Steak vs. soy protein

4   Proteins are large molecules composed of various combinations of 22 smaller compounds called amino acids. The human body, if it has enough raw material, can synthesize most of those amino acids. But eight or nine—called the essential amino acids—cannot be synthesized. They must be supplied in food, and they are needed in certain proportions.

5   Other animals produce proteins whose amino acids are in roughly the same proportion as those required by humans, so protein from animal flesh, milk, and eggs is called complete, or high-quality protein. Wheat germ, dried yeast, and soybeans approach animal protein in quality. But most plant proteins are low in one or more essential amino acids; the deficient (or limiting) amino acid varies from plant to plant.

6   The body doesn't care where its amino acids come from, and few vegetarians eat just one plant food. Most of them eat some animal protein, and most animal protein is complete. Animal protein also improves the quality of plant protein when the two are eaten together— an effect known as protein complementation. Thus, the limiting amino acids in macaroni, shredded wheat, or rye bread are filled in when those foods are eaten as macaroni and cheese, shredded wheat and milk, or an egg-salad sandwich on rye. So ovolacto-vegetarians needn't worry about getting enough good-quality protein.

7   It's also possible to improve the quality of plant protein by combining foods with different limiting amino acids. And because the limiting amino acids of similar plant foods tend to be similar, you don't have to memorize an amino-acid table to complement plant protein. Beans and rice, for example, are a food combination common through- out the world. The limiting amino acid of the beans (methionine) is supplied by the rice, and the limiting amino acid of the rice (lysine) is supplied by the beans. Grains (such as rice, oats, wheat, and corn) and legumes (such as beans, lentils, and peas) complement each other effectively. Combinations can be as mundane as peanut butter sand- wiches or as exotic as tabouli, the cracked-wheat and chickpea salad of the Middle East. Other plant proteins don't complement the protein in grains and legumes quite as well but are still useful as protein sources.

8   Protein malnutrition usually occurs only when you don't get enough food to eat. The person most vulnerable is the young child eating a monotonous all-plant diet. Plant foods are generally bulky and have a low protein content (cooked rice, for example, is only about 2 percent protein). It's therefore sometimes hard for small children to eat enough to meet their protein needs. Even a small amount of animal protein, such as milk, can significantly improve the quality of protein a child eats. Fortified soy milk can also be useful in helping a child get enough high-quality protein.

TURN TO COMPREHENSION CHECK AT END OF CHAPTER

716 words

READING TIMES:
1st reading _____ minutes
2nd reading _____ minutes

READING SPEED:
6 minutes = 119 wpm
5 minutes = 143 wpm
4 minutes = 179 wpm
3 minutes = 239 wpm

A. **Analysis of Ideas and Relationships: Circle the letter next to the best answer.**

1. Paragraph 1 explains:
   a. the function of protein.
   b. why eating protein makes you stronger.
   c. how much protein you should eat every day.

2. According to the chart in paragraph 2:
   a. females need the most protein when they are age _____ .
   b. males age 11–14 need _____ grams of protein.
   c. the group that needs the *least* protein is _____ , age _____ .

3. In paragraph 3, the letters **RDA** stand for:
   a. Recommended Dietary Absorption.
   b. Reasonable Daily Amount.
   c. Recommended Daily Allowance.

4. Read the last sentence in paragraph 3 and all of paragraph 4. Paragraph 4:
   a. is not connected to paragraph 3.
   b. is an explanation of what amino acids are.
   c. gives examples of amino acids mentioned in paragraph 3.

5. According to paragraph 6, **protein complementation** means:
   a. eating lots of high-quality animal protein.
   b. adding some animal protein to a plant protein and eating both together.
   c. avoiding a vegetarian diet.

6. The fourth sentence in paragraph 6 ("Thus, the limiting amino acids . . .") refers back to:
   a. the sentence immediately preceding it.
   b. the first sentence in the paragraph.
   c. the second sentence in the paragraph.

7. The best summary of the information in paragraph 7 is:
   a. food combinations that complement each other.
   b. food combinations that are common throughout the world.
   c. mundane and exotic food combinations.

8. "Other plant proteins don't complement the protein in grains and legumes quite as well but are still useful as protein sources."
   a. Other plant proteins should be avoided since they are poor protein sources.
   b. Other plant proteins can provide some protein, but not as much as grains and legumes.
   c. All plant proteins complement each other equally.

9. In paragraph 8, sentence 2 ("The person most vulnerable . . .") refers to:
   a. plant proteins.
   b. monotonous all-plant diet.
   c. protein malnutrition.

10. The subject of this article is:
    a. how to get enough high-quality protein in your diet.
    b. why you should become a vegetarian.
    c. how to determine your protein RDA.

B. **Interpretation of Words and Phrases: Circle the letter next to the best answer.**

1. "Protein has assumed an almost religious importance in the American diet."
   a. People worship protein instead of practicing a regular religion.
   b. People celebrate religious holidays by eating protein foods.
   c. People are so concerned about protein that they treat it almost like a religion.

2. "The **following** table shows how the RDAs change...."
   a. (the table) that appears next
   b. second
   c. previous

3. According to paragraph 3, why are the RDAs for protein set high?
   a. To allow for individual needs.
   b. To show the effect of controlled studies.
   c. For a margin of safety against deficiency.
   d. both (a) and (b)
   e. both (b) and (c)
   f. both (a) and (c)
   g. (a), (b), and (c)

4. In paragraph 3 ("That amount would be provided . . ."), **that amount** refers to:
   a. a margin of safety against deficiency.
   b. 30–35 grams of protein a day.
   c. 56 grams of protein a day.

5. Other animals produce amino acids in **roughly** the same proportion.
   a. exactly
   b. approximately
   c. scarcely

6. In paragraph 6 ("Most of them eat some animal protein . . ."), **most of them** refers to:
   a. vegetarians.
   b. bodies.
   c. amino acids.

7. The limiting amino acid in macaroni is **filled in** when it is eaten as macaroni and cheese.
   a. lost
   b. substituted
   c. completed

8. Beans and rice **are common** throughout the world.
   a. taste good
   b. are liked
   c. are found everywhere

9. "Plant foods are generally **bulky** . . . ."
   a. easy to digest
   b. of large volume
   c. low in protein

10. "**Even** a small amount . . . can significantly improve the quality of protein a child eats."
    a. Therefore
    b. Equally
    c. Just

C. **Synonyms: From the following list, choose a synonym for the word in bold type in each sentence. Be sure to use correct verb tenses and singular or plural forms for nouns.**

amount	percentage	shortage
to enrich	to provide	to soak up
idea	repetitious and boring	unusual
to make up		

1. People have the **notion** that they need lots of protein.

2. You need amino acids in certain **proportions**.

3. To avoid a calcium **deficiency**, have some cheese or milk every day.

4. How much protein can your body **absorb**?

5. Proteins **are composed** of amino acids.

6. Animal food **supplies** high-quality protein.

7. You can get good nutrition from mundane or **exotic** meals.

8. People who eat a **monotonous** diet probably lack some nutrients.

9. Most plant foods have a low protein **content**.

10. Milk **is fortified** with Vitamin D.

D. Prepositions and Verb-Completers: Write any appropriate preposition or verb-completer in the blank spaces.

1. Protein's primary function _____ the body is the creation _____ tissues.

2. The amount _____ protein you need depends _____ your size and age.

3. The RDAs _____ protein are set high _____ allow _____ a margin _____ safety _____ deficiency.

4. That amount would be provided by as little as four ounces _____ tuna.

5. You have _____ eat enough high-quality protein.

6. Other animals produce protein _____ roughly the same proportion as humans need, so protein _____ animals is called complete.

7. The limiting amino acid varies _____ plant _____ plant.

8. The body doesn't care where its amino acids come _____ .

9. Ovolacto-vegetarians needn't worry _____ getting enough high-quality protein.

10. It's also possible _____ improve the quality _____ plant protein _____ combining foods _____ different limiting amino acids.

E. Antonyms: Each sentence contains two opposite words. Circle the word that completes the sentence correctly.

1. I'm tired of doing the same, old (mundane—exotic) things every day.

2. Mr. Lopez enjoys (strenuous—easy) activities such as mountain climbing.

3. During the war, the soldiers felt very (vulnerable—protected), so they carried their guns all the time.

4. People who eat a (monotonous—varied) diet will get enough nutrients naturally.

5. I had (a deficiency—an overabundance) of apples this year, so I gave some to my neighbors.

6. A good raincoat should (absorb—repel) water effectively.

7. There are (roughly—exactly) 450–460 grams to a pound.

8. That restaurant is rarely crowded so (it's essential to—it doesn't matter if you) have a reservation.

9. That (bulky—small) package just won't fit into my car.

10. Before we begin Chapter 11, let's look back to the (following—previous) chapter.

F.   Graph Reading: Look at the protein graphs and answer these questions.

1. Read the explanation that accompanies the graphs. This information:
   a. shows why rice isn't a complete protein.
   b. is not connected in any way to the graphs.
   c. explains how to read the graphs.

2. On the graphs, why are some portions gray and others white?
   a. The gray shows the pattern for high-quality protein and the white shows deficient areas.
   b. The white shows the pattern for high-quality protein and the gray shows deficient areas.
   c. The gray shows the pattern for cows' milk and the white shows soybeans.

3. Where did you find the information to answer question 2?
   a. It is stated in the note that accompanies the graphs.
   b. There is no explanation given in the graphs.
   c. I looked at the graphs and figured it out myself.

4. According to the explanation and the graphs, which statements are **false**?
   a. If you eat lots of rice, you will eventually get enough lysine.
   b. Soybeans give you complete high-quality protein.
   c. Meat, fish, and eggs also supply complete high-quality protein.
   d. Soybeans will fill in the missing lysine in rice, but cannot fill in the missing tryptophan in corn.

5. What are the words under each column on the graphs?
   a. These are a variety of the amino acids that the body can manufacture by itself.
   b. These are the 8 or 9 essential amino acids that must be supplied by the protein in food.
   c. These are the amino acids that are low quality and must be supplemented by other foods in our diet.

PROTEIN COMPLEMENTATION

In order to make protein, the human body needs eight or nine amino acids that must be supplied by the protein in food. And the body needs those essential amino acids in a certain proportion. If a food is low in one or more of the amino acids, the quality of its protein isn't as high as in a food that supplies all of them in the proper quantities.

We've superimposed the pattern for high-quality protein on the protein patterns (in gray) for five foods. Cows' milk and soybeans meet the pattern (as do meat, fish, and eggs); wheat, corn, and rice fall short. If you ate only one of those three grains, the quality of its protein would not improve, no matter how much you ate.

But by combining foods, the protein patterns can be improved. The extra lysine in milk, say, fills in the lysine missing in rice. That's protein complementation.

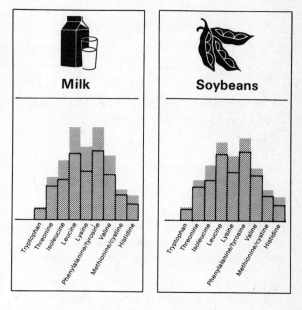

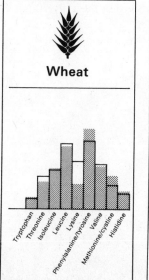

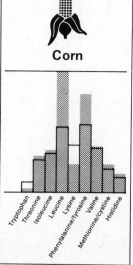

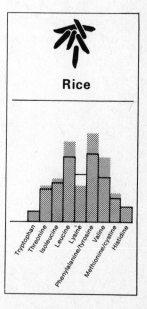

6. An example of protein complementation is:
   a. eating milk with soybeans.
   b. eating corn with wheat.
   c. eating rice with soybeans.

   Why did you choose your answer?

7. Using the graphs, list two other examples of protein complementation.
   a. _____
   b. _____

8. According to the graphs, which essential amino acid would vegetarians have to be most concerned about?
   a. Tryptophan.
   b. Lysine.
   c. Mathionine/cystine.

   Why did you choose your answer?

9. Think of a popular food combination from your native country that exemplifies protein complementation as shown on these graphs.
   a. What is the food combination? _____
   b. What amino acids are complemented? _____

10. Why do you think these five foods were chosen for the graphs?
    a. They are commonly eaten foods that the reader would be interested in knowing about.
    b. They are the only five foods that contain high-quality proteins.
    c. There seems to be no particular reason for choosing these five foods.

    Why did you choose your answer?

G. Word Forms: Choose the correct word form to fit into each sentence. Use appropriate verb tenses, singular or plural forms for nouns, and passive voice where necessary.

Noun	*Verb*	*Adjective*	*Adverb*
approach	to approach	approachable approaching	
determination	to determine	determined	
difference	to differ	different	differently
effect effectiveness	to effect	effective	effectively
essence		essential	essentially
function	to function	functional	functionally
margin		marginal	marginally
occurrence	to occur		
		strenuous	strenuously
variety variation	to vary	various	variously

1. **strenuous, strenuously**
   a. It's good for your health to exercise _____ .
   b. Get involved in _____ exercise.

2. **function, to function, functional, functionally**
   a. I like simple, _____ furniture.
   b. An administrative assistant oversees many different _____ in an office.
   c. & d. Some people _____ best in the morning, while others are _____ more productive in the afternoon.

3. **variety, variation, to vary, various, variously**
   a. I have visited _____ countries in Europe.
   b. Customs _____ in the countries I have visited.
   c. I tried a _____ of new foods in every country.
   d. Spain has an interesting _____ on rice and shellfish called paella.
   e. From time to time, I have _____ worked as a printer, an editor, and an artist.

4. **occurrence, to occur**
   a. A total eclipse of the moon _____ two years from now.
   b. You shouldn't miss such an unusual _____ .

5. **margin, marginal, marginally**
   a. Please don't write beyond the left and right _____ of the page.
   b. The movie was _____ better than the book. Both were poor.
   c. The medicine had a _____ effect on my cold. I'm still sick.

6. **essence, essential, essentially**
   a. It is _____ that you be here by 8 A.M.
   b. _____ , he was against the project because it was expensive.
   c. The _____ of his argument was that the project was too expensive.

7. **approach, to approach, approachable, approaching**
   a. The firemen _____ the burning building carefully.
   b. You can use many _____ to solve the problem.
   c. A good-natured person is always _____ .
   d. The accident occurred because the driver didn't see the _____ bus.

8. **difference, to differ, different, differently**
   a. My brother and I think _____ about movies.
   b. We like _____ types of movies.
   c. One of our _____ is that he likes musicals, and I like science fiction.
   d. We _____ a great deal in other ways too.

9. **effect, effectiveness, to effect, effective, effectively**
   a. Were there any side-_____ from that medicine?
   b. That medicine is _____ against arthritis.
   c. Ms. Bell spoke so _____ that everyone voted for her.
   d. She promised _____ some changes in state government.
   e. You can measure the _____ of her ideas four years from now.

10. **determination, to determine, determined**
    a. Theodore has a lot of _____ to succeed.
    b. We cannot _____ the answer without investigation.
    c. He will succeed with _____ effort.

H. **Sentence Construction: Use each group of words in the given order and form to make an original, meaningful sentence.**

1. protein, assumed, religious, diet

2. protein's, function, creation, tissue

3. quality, protein, determined, amino acids

4. body, care, come from, and, vegetarians, eat

5. for example, common, throughout, world

I. **Topics for Discussion and Composition**

1. This article says that protein has assumed "an almost religious importance" in the American diet. Are there any foods or nutrients that are considered this important in your native country? If there aren't any, explain why not. Give some examples to illustrate your position.

2. Food is very prominent in American advertising on TV and in magazines and newspapers. Compared to your native country, do you notice anything different about what kinds of foods are advertised and how they are described (for example, why, when, and with whom you should eat them; how the foods look; how much you should eat)? Give several examples to illustrate your answer.

3. "You are what you eat." Do you agree with this statement? What does it mean to you? What kinds of foods do you think people should eat? Discuss your opinion by giving several reasons why you agree or disagree with this statement.

4. Do you think there is any connection between what people eat and how they behave? Give several examples to explain your answer.

5. Some people believe that it is good to take lots of vitamins. They feel that vitamins can prevent or cure certain diseases and that vitamins can have a great effect on some body conditions. What is your attitude towards "vitamin therapy"? Discuss your opinion.

6. From your own reading of newspapers and magazines, discuss another recent article that you have seen concerning nutrition or food.

J. Reading Reconstruction: Read this paragraph as many times as you can in three minutes. Then, with your book closed, try to restate the ideas in writing as clearly and completely as you can. (See exercise J in Chapter 1 for complete instructions.)

Do you Need Extra Vitamins?

Vitamins and minerals are essential for good health. A varied, balanced diet usually supplies a full complement of all the nutrients you need. Vitamin deficiencies rarely occur in the United States, but some people still worry about deficiencies and believe that they will be healthier if they take extra vitamins. Other people feel that extra vitamins are effective in curing or preventing diseases. What can happen if you take large amounts of vitamins? In most cases, vitamins are absorbed in the correct proportions and the rest leave the body. However, Vitamins A and D remain in the fat tissue and can result in vitamin poisoning. The full effect of vitamins on the body has not been determined, and some experts question whether we need to fortify ourselves with extra vitamins.

Key words (to be written on the chalkboard):

vitamins	nutrients	large amounts
minerals	vitamin deficiencies	absorbed
essential	rarely	vitamin poisoning
health	the United States	effect
varied, balanced diet	extra vitamins	not determined

Comprehension Check

On a separate piece of paper, write the numbers 1 through 10 on both sides. Mark one side "Test 1" and the other side "Test 2." Read each statement and decide whether it is true or false. Write "T" after true statements and "F" after false statements under Test 1. After you have finished the comprehension check, turn Test 1 face down. Then read the article again and do the comprehension check again under Test 2. Base your answers on the information in this article *only*, even if you disagree with what the author said.

1. Eating more protein makes you stronger.

2. The major function of protein is to create and repair body tissue.

3. An average man needs the same amount of protein as an average woman.

4. RDAs for protein have been set at very minimal levels.

5. All protein, whether from plants or animals, is high-quality protein.

6. Proteins are composed of various combinations of amino acids.

7. Eight or nine essential amino acids must be supplied in the foods we eat.

8. Animal proteins are all high-quality proteins.

9. The body must get its amino acids from specific foods.

10. You can combine different foods to improve the quality of their proteins.

12

Before you read, here are some questions to think about:

— Have you ever been close to death?

— How did you survive?

— Do you think belief in recovery and the will to live are important factors in healing?

— Do you think belief and healing are related? Why? Or why not?

THE HEALING POWER
OF BELIEF

[The medical profession is beginning to learn that what people *believe* strongly affects their state of being. Here's a report by an expert who has been studying the mind-body effect at the UCLA (University of California in Los Angeles) medical school. Norman Cousins is the author of *Human Options*, from which this article was drawn. *Human Options* was published by W. W. Norton & Co., Inc. in 1982.]

1   For the past two years, I have been studying cancer survivors at UCLA, trying to find out why it is that some people respond much better to their treatment than do others. At first I thought that some patients did well because their illnesses were not as severe as the illnesses of others. On closer scrutiny, however, I discovered that severity of the illness was only one of a number of factors that accounted for the difference between those who get well and those who don't. The patients I am talking about here received upon diagnosis whatever therapy— medication, radiation, surgery—their individual cases demanded. Yet the response to such treatments was hardly uniform. Some patients fared much better in their therapies than others.

2   What was it, then, that was different? Was there any one thing that *all* survivors had in common? Yes. I have found that the major characteristics of these survivors were very similar. Among the similarities are:

- They all had a strong will to live.
- They were not panicky about their illness.
- They had confidence in their ability to persevere.
- Despite all the forecasts to the contrary, they believed they could make it.
- They were capable of joyous response.
- They were convinced that their treatment would work.

Annie's story

3   One woman with whom I worked closely is perhaps symbolic of the entire group. Let's call her Annie. Her illness was diagnosed as cancer of the liver. An exploratory operation convinced the surgeons

that the disease was too far along to be treated by any known means. But Annie, far from being discouraged or depressed by this verdict, was absolutely determined to overcome her illness. She decided to fight with all of her powers of mind and body. Her family physician was so impressed with her spirit that he felt the dismal prediction of the specialists ought not to preclude further efforts. Very supportive, he encouraged Annie to see a surgeon in Houston who had a high record of success with patients who had a strong will to live and a confident attitude. The surgeon's name was John Stehlin.

4   Annie went to Houston and was interviewed by Dr. Stehlin. She visited the floor in St. Joseph's Hospital where Dr. Stehlin's patients were cared for. Instead of a gloomy white hospital setting, she found a cheerful, animated, attractive series of rooms, the largest of which was called the Living Room. It was equipped with easy chairs, reading corners, and alcoves for audio-video machines, containing a large array of tape cassettes of some of the funniest motion pictures ever produced. Dr. Stehlin installed the sets and obtained the cassettes after reading an article I wrote for the *New England Journal of Medicine* on the therapeutic value of laughter. He had always believed that hopefulness and laughter go together. People who are capable of experiencing joy, he discovered, were much better candidates for successful surgery and therapy than those who were morbid and apprehensive.

5   After spending only 15 minutes with Dr. Stehlin, Annie felt uplifted and thrilled by the atmosphere of the place. She met with patients who had come through even greater ordeals than her own. Dr. Stehlin examined Annie and studied her medical record. Then he told her he would be willing to operate and give her the best possible care—but only if she had complete confidence in herself, in him, and in the operation. He suggested that she return home to think about it.

6   Annie did, but there wasn't much to think about. She was eager to proceed. When she returned to Houston, it was obvious to Dr. Stehlin that she was strongly motivated. He operated and removed 70 percent of her liver. Nevertheless, Annie's convalescence at St. Joseph's was rapid. She was caught up in a powerful, affirmative atmosphere. Today, three years later, she is active and free of symptoms. Annie and Dr. Stehlin know the odds are that there are probably other pockets of cancer throughout her body. But her condition has stabilized. She is a happy, functioning human being.

Powers of the mind

7   At the School of Medicine of the University of California, Los Angeles, I have been trying to find out if emotions affect the chemistry of the human body. For several decades, the term "psychosomatic" has been in general use. It means mind-body relationship. But the precise

way the mind affects the body has not been clearly defined. As the result of recent research, however, it is possible to say that specific changes take place throughout the body as the result of human attitudes.

8   Indeed, Dr. Richard Bergland, a brain researcher at the Harvard Medical School, has written a paper suggesting that the human brain is basically a gland. Building on this view, Dr. Carmine Clemente, director of the Brain Research Institute at UCLA, has been looking into the secretions of the brain. He has estimated that there may be thousands of such secretions—all of which play a part in the functioning of the body.

9   What to me is most fascinating of all about these secretions is that they are not locked away or completely removed from the conscious intelligence. It is true that the mind has no ongoing awareness of the numberless functions generated by the brain—the beating of the heart, the actions of the nerve cells, the functions of all the glands. But the fact that we have no *direct* knowledge of these functions as they occur does not mean that we are barred from any supervision over them. The significance of biofeedback—a term used to describe the ability of the mind to enter into the workings of the body—is that human beings may actually be able to exert increasing control over themselves and may be able to play an important role in overcoming illness.

10   Numerous medical reports now cite instances in which individuals have been able to direct their bodies in ways generally believed to be beyond the reach of the conscious intelligence. At the UCLA School of Medicine, I witnessed a demonstration in which a man controlled his own heartbeat. He could speed it up or slow it almost to a stop merely by concentrating. Such a performance is not unknown in Eastern cultures, but it was startling, to say the least, to see such a demonstration in an American medical school, with a dozen or more physicians as fascinated observers of this use of biofeedback. Patients are using biofeedback techniques at the Menninger Foundation in Topeka, Kansas, and at other medical centers as a means of relieving their migraine headaches or lowering their blood pressure. The evidence is incontrovertible that chemical changes take place in the body as a result of mental functions or moods.

The placebo effect

11   This mind-body effect should not be surprising in view of the experience over the years with placebos. The term "placebo" is used to describe a "pill" that contains no medical ingredients but that often produces the same effect as genuine medication. Placebos provide ample proof that expectations can have an effect on body chemistry. According to a recent article on placebos in *Medical World News*, studies conducted over the past 25 years have shown that placebos satisfactorily relieved symptoms in an average of 35 percent of patients tested. These

symptoms include: fever, severe postoperative pain, anginal pain, headache, and anxiety, among other complaints. The explanation for this strange phenomenon is that the human mind can create actual changes in body chemistry as a result of what it *believes*. If, for example, a person believes that a certain medication contains a substance that can accomplish a specific need, the body tends to move in that direction.

12   An increasing number of scientists now contend that the body's healing system and its belief system are closely related. That is why hope, faith, and the will to live can be vital factors in the war against disease. The belief system converts positive expectations into plus factors in any contest against illness.

A doctor's best medicine

13   Another crucial factor that influences the system of belief and healing is the attitude of the physician. One of a doctor's main functions is to engage to the fullest the patient's own ability to mobilize the forces of mind and body in turning back disease. The patient's belief in the judgment and healing power of the physician is often more important than the treatment itself in reversing the course of the illness. Dr. Herbert Benson, an associate professor of medicine at Harvard Medical School and author of *The Mind-Body Effect*, believes that a doctor's "caring" about his or her patient causes specific physiological improvement. In Annie's case, for example, she had a very supportive family physician plus the enlightened Dr. Stehlin, who was very aware that encouragement and a positive attitude can be all-important.

14   People who are seriously ill need to believe that they have a chance. They respond not just to the doctor's attitude but to the mood of the people very close to them. If hope is missing from the eyes and from the voices of their families, the absence will be felt. I feel that in the future there will be more and more programs in which caring professionals will help patients and their families to cope and to support the ill person and each other.

The positive effects of laughter

15   It makes no sense to believe that only the negative emotions have an effect on the body's chemistry. Every emotion, negative or positive, makes its registrations on the body's systems. When I was ill, I read every humorous book I could get my hands on. My goal was to be uplifted and relieved of worry and panic through laughter. That's why Dr. Stehlin uses comic films as part of his therapy. Illness is not a laughing matter, but perhaps it ought to be. Laughter is a form of internal jogging. It moves the organs around. It enhances respiration. It is an igniter of great expectations.

16   Through my studies at the medical school and from my own experience, I have learned that one of the prime elements of human uniqueness is the ability to create and exercise new options. What an individual decides to do with his or her life; what a person believes or doesn't believe about the great mysteries of life; how people go about fulfilling their individual and collective needs and desires—all these involve options. Protecting and cherishing our right to exercise these options may well represent the finest example of true human freedom.

17   We must learn never to underestimate the capacity of the human mind and body to regenerate—even when the prospects seem most wretched. The life-force may be the least understood force on earth. The eminent psychologist and philosopher William James said that human beings tend to live too much within self-imposed limits. It is possible that these limits will recede when we respect more fully the natural drive of the human mind and body toward perfectibility and regeneration.

18   The most important thing I have learned about the power of belief is that an individual patient's attitude toward serious illness can be as important as medical help. It would be a serious mistake to bypass or minimize the need for scientific treatment, but that treatment will be far more effective if people put their creative hopes, their faith, and their confidence fully to work in behalf of their recovery.

TURN TO COMPREHENSION CHECK AT END OF CHAPTER

1800 words

READING TIMES:
1st reading _____ minutes
2nd reading_____ minutes

READING SPEED:
15 minutes = 120 wpm
12 minutes = 150 wpm
10 minutes = 180 wpm
 8 minutes = 225 wpm
 6 minutes = 300 wpm

A. **Analysis of Ideas and Relationships: Circle the letter next to the best answer.**

1. The main point of this article is that:
   a. a patient's belief that he or she can recover can be as important as medical treatment.
   b. medical treatment is unnecessary if a patient has a strong will to live.
   c. there are many new treatments for cancer, and cancer no longer has to be fatal.

   Please explain your answer.

2. One of the things Norman Cousins, the author, is interested in is finding out:
   a. why some patients respond better to treatment than others do.
   b. which treatments (medication, radiation, surgery) are most effective.
   c. the causes of cancer and early means of detecting it.

3. Mr. Cousins uses Annie as an example of:
   a. a person with a severe form of cancer and a poor prognosis for survival.
   b. a seriously ill person who was absolutely determined to overcome her illness.
   c. a seriously ill person who had a negative attitude toward treatment and a morbid outlook on life in general.

   Please explain your answer.

4. Mr. Cousins stresses the importance in healing of:
   a. a cheerful, attractive environment.
   b. laughter.
   c. the patient's belief in recovery.
   d. the doctor's belief in recovery.
   e. all of the above.

5. Which statement is NOT true?
   a. The mind can control the body.
   b. All emotions, positive and negative, have an effect on the body's systems.
   c. There is no place for laughter when dealing with serious illness.

6. The placebo effect is important (paragraph 11) because it demonstrates:
   a. that pills are not necessary and don't do any good.
   b. the power of the mind's expectations over body chemistry.
   c. that most people don't know or can't tell what they are taking.

   Please explain your answer.

7. Paragraph 13 is about:
   a. the importance of having a technically skilled physician.
   b. Dr. Herbert Benson, associate professor of medicine at Harvard.
   c. the importance of the attitude of the physician in the healing.

8. Put the following statements into logical order. Then refer to paragraph 16 to check your work.
   a. "Protecting and cherishing our right to exercise these options may well represent the finest example of true human freedom."
   b. "Through my studies at the medical school and from my own experience, I have learned that one of the prime elements of human uniqueness is the ability to create and exercise new options."
   c. "What an individual decides to do with his or her life; what a person believes or doesn't believe about the great mysteries of life; how people go about fulfilling their individual and collective needs and desires—all these involve options."

9. The tone of this article is:
   a. positive and hopeful.
   b. neutral and emotionally low-keyed.
   c. negative and critical of current medical practices.

   Why do you think so?

10. If you were very seriously ill and you asked Mr. Cousins for advice, what do you think he would tell you to do?
    a. Get your worldly affairs in order, forgive your enemies, and calmly prepare for death.
    b. Get the most competent medical treatment available and leave your fate to the experts.
    c. Never give up your will to live, find a doctor who believes that you can recover, and get the best medical treatment available.

    Why do you think so?

B. Interpretation of Words and Phrases: Circle the letter next to the best answer.

1. "Was there any one thing that all survivors had in common?"
   a. In what way were all the people who recovered alike?
   b. In what way were all the people who recovered different?
   c. In what way were the people who did not recover alike?

2. "Despite all the forecasts to the contrary, they [the survivors] believed they could make it."
   a. Even though the medical predictions were against recovery, the people who survived believed that they could recover.
   b. The favorable medical predictions helped the people who survived believe that they could recover.
   c. The unfavorable medical predictions discouraged people from believing they could recover.

3. "... the disease was **too far along** to be treated by any known means."
   a. too far away
   b. too far advanced
   c. too unfamiliar

4. "... he felt the dismal predictions of the specialists ought not to preclude further efforts."
   a. He felt that other treatments should be explored even though the specialists did not believe recovery was possible.
   b. He felt that there was no use in trying other treatments because the specialists did not believe recovery was possible.
   c. He felt that the specialists were definitely wrong in their diagnosis and that the disease was not as advanced as they said.

5. "[Dr. Stehlin] suggested that [Annie] return home to think about it. Annie did, but **there wasn't much to think about**." (See paragraph 5 and the beginning of paragraph 6 for context.)
   a. There wasn't much to think about because Annie had no intentions of undergoing the treatment he recommended.
   b. There wasn't much to think about because Annie didn't have enough information to be able to make a decision about the treatment.
   c. There wasn't much to think about then because Annie had already thought about it and made her decision to participate in the treatment he recommended.

6. "[Annie] was **caught up in** a powerful, affirmative atmosphere."
   a. trapped in
   b. completely involved in
   c. taken in by

7. "The evidence is incontrovertible that chemical changes take place in the body as a result of mental functions or moods."
   a. There is no question that the mind causes chemical changes in the body.
   b. There is some evidence to suggest that the mind causes chemical changes in the body.
   c. There is no evidence to suggest that the mind causes chemical changes in the body.

8. "Dr. Herbert Benson, an associate professor of medicine at Harvard Medical School and author of *the Mind-Body Effect,* believes that a doctor's 'caring' about his or her patient causes specific physiological improvement." Dr. Benson believes that:
   a. a patient gets better if the doctor really cares about him or her.
   b. whether or not a doctor really cares about a patient is not important in treatment. It's only the treatment that is important.
   c. if a doctor really cares about a patient, it is important for the patient emotionally but not physiologically.

9. "Illness is not a laughing matter, but perhaps it ought to be." By this, Mr. Cousins means:
   a. people take illness too seriously.
   b. illness is a very serious matter, but seriously ill patients feel more positive and optimistic if they relieve their worry and panic by laughing.
   c. illness cannot be helped, so patients might as well make the best of it and try to be cheerful.

10. ". . . one of the prime elements of human uniqueness is the ability to create and exercise new options."
    a. One of the main ways people are different from other animals is that people are able to think up and act out new life choices.
    b. People are like other animals in that they are limited in the life choices they can make.
    c. People, unlike other animals, are not able to think up and act out new life choices.

C. **Synonyms: From this list choose a synonym for the word in bold type in each sentence. Be sure to use correct verb tenses and singular or plural forms for nouns.**

to fight	in spite of
to get along	prediction
to continue to make a great effort	chance (of recovery)
to rebuild (themselves)	full of anxiety
negative and depressing	the same

1. Seriously ill people do not have **uniform** reactions to their situation.

2. Some **fare** better in treatment than others do.

3. It is important for very ill people not to become **panicky.**

4. It is also important to **persevere** in treatment and not to give up.

5. & 6. Some people recover completely **despite** the medical **prognosis.**

7. These people have tried to remain cheerful and not give in to **morbid** thoughts.

8. They **have struggled** to keep their will to live.

9. They have never lost hope even when **the odds** have been against them.

10. The human mind and body have a great capacity to **regenerate.**

D. **Prepositions and Verb-Completers: Write any appropriate preposition or verb-completer in the blank spaces.**

1. The severity _____ the illness was only one _____ a number _____ factors that accounted _____ the difference _____ those who get well and those who don't.

2. What did the survivors have _____ common?

3. The major characteristics _____ these survivors were very similar.

4. They all had a strong will _____ live.

5. They were not panicky _____ their illness.

6. They had confidence _____ their ability _____ persevere and _____ overcome their illness.

7. Mr. Cousins is interested _____ finding _____ if the emotions affect the chemistry _____ the human body.

8. He believes _____ the therapeutic value _____ laughter.

9. Mr. Cousins believes that the power _____ belief is _____ great importance _____ the healing process.

10. He says, however, that it would be a serious mistake _____ bypass or minimize the need _____ scientific treatment.

E. Cloze Exercise: Select the best word to fill in each blank. Sometimes there may be more than one possible answer.

For the past two years, I have been studying cancer survivors at UCLA, trying to find out why it is that some people respond much better to their treatment than do others. At first I thought that (1)_____ (some—many—all) patients did well because their (2)_____ (illnesses—sicknesses—treatments) were not as severe as (3)_____ (these—the—those) illnesses of others. On closer (4)_____ (see—watch—scrutiny), however, I discovered that severity (5)_____ (with—for—of) the illness was only one (6)_____ (more—of—with) a number of factors that (7)_____ (accounted—did—stood) for the difference between those (8)_____ (that—which—who) get well and those who (9)_____ (didn't—don't—won't). The patients I am talking about (10)_____ (here—later—before) received upon diagnosis whatever therapy—(11)_____ (treatment—medication—therapy), radiation, surgery— their individual cases (12)_____ (asked—called—demanded). Yet the response to such (13)_____ (conditions—cases—treatments) was hardly uniform. Some patients (14)_____ (were—followed—fared) much better in their therapies than others.

F. **Punctuation Exercise: Write in capital letters, periods, question marks, colons, and commas where needed.**

what was it then that was different was there any one thing that all survivors had in common yes i have found that the major characteristics of these survivors were very similar among the similarities are they all had a strong will to live they were not panicky about their illness they had confidence in their ability to persevere despite all the forecasts to the contrary they believed they could make it they were capable of joyous response they were convinced that their treatment would work

G. **Word Forms: Choose the correct word form to fit into each sentence referring to the chart as necessary. Use appropriate verb tenses, singular or plural forms for nouns, and passive voice where necessary.**

Noun	*Verb*	*Adjective*	*Adverb*
character characteristic characterization	to characterize	characteristic	characteristically
confidant confidence confidentiality	to confide	confident confidential	confidentially
explorer exploratory exploration	to explore	exploratory	
laughter laugh	to laugh	laughing	laughingly
limit limitation	to limit	limiting limited	
response	to respond	responsive	responsively
severity		severe	severely
success	to succeed	successful	successfully
survivor survival	to survive	surviving	
will willingness	to will	willing	willingly

1. **survivor, survival, to survive, surviving**
   a. How many people _____ the crash?
   b. Were there many _____ ?
   c. Do you believe in the _____ of the fittest?
   d. The _____ spouse will inherit the estate.

2. **success, to succeed, successful, successfully**
   a. She was _____ in her fight against cancer.
   b. She _____ in her fight.
   c. He wished her every _____ .
   d. I am glad to say that I handled the situation _____ .

3. **laughter, laugh, to laugh, laughing, laughingly**
   a. The children _____ when they saw the clown.
   b. He had a hearty _____ , and you could hear him far away.
   c. This is no _____ matter; you must be serious.
   d. "Oh, I'm sure you'll understand," he said _____ .
   e. The room was full of _____ and happiness.

4. **will, willingness, to will, willing, willingly**
   a. I would _____ do anything I could for him.
   b. He is very ill, but he may recover because he has the _____ to live.
   c. He _____ himself to recover.
   d. I am ready, _____ and able to help you.
   e. Do you doubt my _____ to carry out the project?

5. **severity, severe, severely**
   a. The judge gave the defendant a _____ sentence.
   b. She was _____ injured in the accident.
   c. The doctor wasn't certain about the _____ of her injuries at first.

6. **response, to respond, responsive, responsively**
   a. I have no _____ to your accusations.
   b. Would you care to _____ to this question?
   c. She may have had the information, but she was not _____ when we asked her for it.
   d. Later she answered _____ .

7. **character, characteristic, characterization, to characterize, characteristic, characteristically**
   a. That writer has a great gift for _____ .
   b. This man has a number of unpleasant _____ .
   c. I have some serious questions about his _____ .
   d. How would you _____ his behavior?
   e. His _____ behavior did not inspire confidence.
   f. He is _____ untrustworthy and unethical.

8. confidant, confidence, confidentiality, to confide, confident, confidential, confidentially
   a. He is an old friend and my closest _____ .
   b. This information is marked _____ .
   c. I have the greatest _____ in her.
   d. I cannot comment because she told me the story in _____ .
   e. She told me _____ .
   f. _____ is absolutely essential because of the nature of the negotiations.
   g. I am _____ in your ability.

9. explorer, exploratory, exploration, to explore, exploratory
   a. It is necessary to _____ this matter in more detail.
   b. The doctor recommended _____ surgery to find the source of the problem.
   c. Marco Polo was a famous _____ .
   d. That book is an _____ of current medical practices.
   e. I am going into the hospital for an _____ tomorrow.

10. limit, limitation, to limit, limiting, limited
   a. I had _____ use for him.
   b. That is the _____ ; I quit!
   c. There are a few _____ spelled out in the agreement.
   d. I will _____ myself to just a few remarks.
   e. Are there any _____ factors?

H. Sentence Paraphrase: Make new sentences using these sentence frames, and then make up your own sentences. You may add or leave out words, but try to retain the meaning of the original sentence.

1. What you believe may affect your state of being, according to Norman Cousins.

   Norman Cousins _____ your state _____

   _____.

   Other possible sentences:

2. The major characteristics of the survivors were very similar, and they included having a strong will to live, not being panicky about their illness, having confidence in their ability to persevere, believing they could make it despite all forecasts to the contrary, being capable of joyous response, and being convinced that their treatment would work.

   The major characteristics of the survivors were very similar:

   • They had a strong will to live.

   • They were not panicky _____.

   • _____.

   • _____.

   • _____.

   • _____.

   Other possible sentences:

3. Another crucial factor that influences the system of belief and healing is the attitude of the physician.

   The attitude _____

   _____.

   Other possible sentences:

I. Topics for Discussion and Composition

1. What place do you think faith, hope, and the will to live have in overcoming illness? Have you ever known anyone who had an extraordinary will to live? If so, describe this person and the situation he or she was in. What finally happened? Did you learn anything from this person's experience?

2. Do you think the mind can control the body? If so, give specific examples. Have you ever tried to control your body through mental concentration? Describe the situation and what you did.

3. Norman Cousins, the author, says that laughter is therapeutic. What do you think he means? Do you agree? Give examples to support your position.

4. Do you believe in fate: for example, that people are destined to live a certain length of time? Do you believe that people can control their destiny? Can you think of specific ways people try to control their destiny? Give specific examples.

5. Do you think that life, no matter what the circumstances, is always preferable to death? Why? Or why not? Can you think of situations where you would choose death over life? If so, describe these situations specifically.

6. Have you ever had a near-death experience? If so, describe the situation. What happened? Why were you dying? How did you feel? What were your thoughts? What caused you to recover? Has this experience changed your life in any way? If so, how? Why?

7. Do you think death should be openly discussed with a dying person? Why? Or why not? How do you want to face your own death? Do you want to be aware of it and to talk about it openly? If so, who would you want to talk to and why?

8. Do you think a person should be able to decide when and how to die? Why? Or why not? Give specific reasons and examples to support your position.

J. **Reading Reconstruction: Read this paragraph as many times as you can in three minutes. Then, with your book closed, try to restate the ideas in writing as clearly and completely as you can. (See exercise J in Chapter 1 for complete instructions.)**

Back from Death

It started out to be a simple exploratory operation. Then, suddenly, the patient's heart stopped. Her brain waves started leveling off. The medical team immediately began emergency treatment to try to start the heart again. At last the chief surgeon announced that the patient had died. Minutes later, much to everyone's amazement, the "dead" patient came back to life. Her heart started, and her brain waves began to assume normal patterns. Later she told the doctors that she had been fully aware of everything that had happened while she was "dead." She believed that she came back to life because she wanted so badly to live longer. She said death was not frightening, but she wasn't ready to go yet. The experts admit that they have no satisfactory explanations for these death or near-death experiences. They admit that they do not fully understand life—and they do not fully understand death.

Key words (to be written on the chalkboard):

death	leveling off	life
exploratory	emergency	assume
operation	treatment	normal patterns
patient	chief surgeon	aware
heart	amazement	near-death experience
brain waves		

Comprehension Check

On a separate piece of paper, write the numbers 1 through 10 on both sides. Mark one side "Test 1" and the other side "Test 2." Read each statement and decide whether it is true or false. Write "T" after true statements and "F" after false statements under Test 1. After you have finished the comprehension check, turn Test 1 face down. Then read the article again and do the comprehension check again under Test 2. Base your answers on the information in this article *only,* even if you disagree with what the author said.

1. The author of this article believes that the patient's attitude is a very important factor in healing.

2. The patient called Annie was suffering from an advanced stage of cancer.

3. The prospects for Annie's recovery were considered to be very poor.

4. Annie was discouraged by the results of the exploratory surgery and felt completely overcome by her illness.

5. Her family physician discouraged her from seeking other medical advice.

6. Annie was very impressed with the positive atmosphere of the treatment center in Houston, Texas, and with Dr. Stehlin.

7. Annie survived the operation, recovered quickly, and three years after surgery, she was leading an active, happy life.

8. More and more scientists believe that the body's healing system and its belief system are closely connected.

9. The author is pessimistic about people and their power to control their minds and bodies.

10. The author states that medical treatment is unnecessary if the patient believes strongly enough in recovery.

Review Examination III (Chapters 9, 10, 11, and 12)

A. Content Summary: Complete these statements and give explanations as asked. (20 points: 5 points each)

1. The main idea of "Indo-European Languages" is:

2. List some ways that American grandmothers of today are different from American grandmothers of the past:

3. Is it necessary to eat meat to get the minimum daily requirement of protein? Explain your answer.

4. Explain the title "The Healing Power of Belief."

B. Word Forms: Look at the first word in each line. Write the appropriate form of this word in the sentence that follows it. Be careful to use appropriate verb tenses, singular and plural forms for nouns, and passive voice where necessary. (40 points: 2 points each)

(Example)

care   Please be *careful* . That package is heavy.

1. origin   Where did the _____ Indo-Europeans live, and what was the nature of their culture?

2. conclude   It is possible to draw certain _____ about the Indo-Europeans and their language.

3. base   _____ , most of the languages in modern-day Europe come from a common origin.

4. assumption   We have a number of reasons for _____ that they descended from the same parent language.

5. designation We can assume that a word that is similar in most of the Indo-European languages _____ a concept that existed in the original Indo-European society.

6. behavior   American grandmothers of today _____ differently than they did in the past.

7. imposition   Sometimes they feel _____ upon when their adult children expect them to baby-sit.

8. professional Many of these grandmothers are quite busy because they have their own careers and _____ .

9. resent   They feel _____ when their children don't recognize how busy they are.

10. **press**   American grandmothers of today are under a lot of _____ .

11. **vary**   It is important to eat a _____ of foods in order to get enough protein.

12. **strenuous**   It is not true that you need more protein when you exercise _____ .

13. **functional** Protein's primary _____ is the creation and repair of tissue.

14. **essence**   _____ , the amount of protein you need depends more on your size and age than on your activity.

15. **different**   People _____ over the best sources of protein, but they all agree that protein is essential to health.

16. **willing**   Norman Cousins believes that the patient's _____ to recover is very important in healing.

17. **survive**   Mr. Cousins is interested in the characteristics of the _____ of serious illnesses.

18. **exploratory** He _____ the differences between those who survive and those who don't survive.

19. **success**   How do some people overcome serious illness and disease _____ ?

20. **confide**   It is important to be _____ in your ability to recover.

C. **Cloze: Choose the most appropriate word for each blank. (10 points: 1 point each)**

Protein has assumed an almost religious importance in the American

diet. Some people still believe (1)_____ eating protein makes
                                    (that—if—because)

you (2)_____ and that strenuous exercise
       (stronger—smarter—bigger)

(3)_____ eating extra protein, though
   (needs—requires—causes)

(4)_____ notions were disproved long (5)_____ .
   (the—some—those)   (time—ago—after)

Protein's primary function in (6)_____ body is the creation
                                 (a—the—this)

(7)_____ repair of tissue—from (8)_____ , muscles, and
   (or—and—for)   (bones—skin—the)

bones to (9)_____ and toenails. The amount
            (hair—muscles—tissue)

(10)_____ protein you need, therefore, depends more on your size and
    (of—in—for)

age than on your activity.

D. Composition: Write a composition about *one* of these topics. (30 points)

1. Compare American grandmothers of today with grandmothers in your country. How are they similar? How are they different? How important do you think grandmothers are? Why? How do they affect society? How important do you think the grandmother-grandchildren relationship is? Why? Give specific examples.

2. Discuss the typical diet of your country and explain its health value. What are the most common sources of protein? Do most people eat meat and, if so, what kinds? What kinds of vegetables do people eat? Do adults drink milk? Do they eat cheese or yogurt?

3. Norman Cousins talks about the importance of the patient having confidence in his or her doctor—and the importance of the doctor believing in the patient's ability to survive. Do people in your country believe that these two areas of confidence are necessary? If so, explain why. What is the typical relationship between patient and doctor in your country? Give examples.

CREDITS

2 Billion More People by Century's End © 1980, U.S. News & World Report, Inc. Reprinted with permission. 8/18/80 issue. Photograph: "People jammed in like sardines" by H. Armstrong Roberts. USN & WR charts—Basic data: United Nations.

Islamic Customs Limit Kuwaiti Women by Thomas L. Friedman. © UPI, 1981. Reprinted with permission. Photograph: "Arab woman health worker" by The United Nations, Monkmeyer Press Photo Service, N.Y., N.Y. Dictionary: from *Oxford American Dictionary* edited by Eugene Ehrlich et al. © 1980 by Oxford University Press, Inc. Reprinted by permission.

How to Cope with Insomnia by Katherine Balfour. © Family Circle. Reprinted by permission. 5/9/81 edition. Photograph: "Insomnia strikes again." Courtesy of Katsushige Hirasawa.

Conversations with a Gorilla © 1978, National Geographic. Reprinted with permission. 10/78 issue. Photograph: "Koko" by Dr. Ronald H. Cohn—The Gorilla Foundation.

How to Find a Job © 1982 International Paper Company. Reprinted with permission. Photograph: "Interview" by Steve Patton.

Made in Japan: A Day in the Life of a Japanese Worker © 1981, Trans World Airlines, Inc. Reprinted from TWA AMBASSADOR with permission of author and publisher. Photograph: "The Morita family" by Akira Suwa/The Philadelphia Inquirer.

Body Language by Flora Davis from INSIDE INTUITION © McGraw-Hill, Inc., 1973. Reprinted by permission. Photograph: "Women and children at a bus stop in San Sebastian, Spain" by Beryl Goldberg.